NEW ENGLAND

BY MAIL

NEW ENGLAND

BY MAIL

Compiled by Daniel and Lisa Ramus

Edited by Ramona Pope Richards

RUTLEDGE HILL PRESS

NASHVILLE, TENNESSEE

Published by Rutledge Hill Press, Inc., 513 Third Avenue South, Nashville, Tennessee 37210

Designed by Harriette Bateman

Library of Congress Cataloging-in-Publication Data

Ramus, Daniel, 1960-
   New England by mail / complied by Daniel and Lisa Ramus ; edited by Ramona Pope Richards
     p. cm.
   Includes index.
   ISBN 1-55853-060-6
   1. Mail-order business—New England—Directories. 2. Handicraft industries—New England—Directories. I. Ramus, Lisa, 1958- . II. Richards, Ramona Pope. III. Title.
HF5466.R36 1990
381'.142'02574—dc20   90-39056
                                               CIP

Printed in the United States of America
1 2 3 4 5 6 7 8 — 95 94 93 92 91 90

CONTENTS

INTRODUCTION

Welcome to New England! The rolling hills of the Berkshires, the harsh weather of the Green Mountains, the stark beauty of the rocky coast of Maine, and the autumn foliage that draws visitors from all over the country are home to a hard-working people that have a reputation for pride in the quality of their work.

New England By Mail includes a collection of companies that carry on the New England heritage of providing quality products at reasonable prices with excellent service. They provide an alternative to mass-produced products that fall apart quickly. Many of these companies have intentionally remained small in order to maintain a personal contact with their customers. Others have expanded slowly and take pride in their service and selection. Some are family-owned businesses that have been in New England for several generations. Others have come to New England, seeing it as the ideal place to live and work.

The purpose of *New England By Mail* is to provide the opportunity to become familiar with some of the finest products New England has to offer. The book is divided into six categories:

Eat, Drink, and Be Merry—The Food Specialties of New England
As You Like It—Homes and Home Furnishings
Putting on the Ritz—New England Crafted Clothing and Personal Accessories
For Kids of All Ages—Hobbies, Crafts, and Toys
Adventures in New England—Travel Opportunities and Unique Vacations
The Unusual and the Unique—Let's Not Forget Anybody

Companies are listed in the category that best describes the majority of their products. Companies that also carry additional product lines will be cross-referenced under that product in the index. Some companies, such as L. L. Bean or The Orvis Company, carry a broad selection of many products. These have been grouped in the last chapter, along with companies that have unusual products that don't fit any of the other five categories.

There is also an appendix with an alphabetical list of all companies included, and an appendix listing the companies by state.

New England By Mail is not designed to give you all the information you need to buy the products mentioned. Its purpose is to introduce you to these companies so that you can get catalogs from those which interest you. Some companies distribute their catalogs free; others charge a fee for them. These fees are often refundable when you place an order, but do not assume that is so unless the company tells you.

Some items mentioned here require you to custom order products to your specifications. When requesting prices on such items, make sure your letter includes as much information as you can provide—size, color, and so forth—and be sure to ask how long the company will honor the price you are given. If you are requesting a price quotation over the telephone, have all the information ready before making the call. Take notes on your conversation since it may be the only tangible record you have.

When placing an order by phone, make sure you know whether or not an item is out of stock, when your order will be shipped, whether any of the items will be shipped separately, and details of the company's return policy. It is also a good idea to get the name or number of the operator who takes your order in case you have questions later. If the operator asks for your phone number, this is generally for your protection to make sure that the order is not being placed on a stolen card with illegally obtained information.

When you order goods by phone or mail, you have entered into a contract of sale. You do not have the right to call and cancel the order or stop payment on a check or money order. States vary concerning the laws in this matter, but trying to cancel your order when not permitted by the company's policies could give the firm cause to bring legal action against you.

The Federal Trade Commission states that a company must ship goods within 30 days of receiving a properly completed written order, unless another date is stated in its catalog or in other information, such as a written quotation on a custom order. Note that the rule states that goods must be *shipped* within 30 days, not delivered.

That 30-day time period starts when the company receives your check or money order or charges your credit card account following the receipt of a written order. Orders placed by telephone and charged to a credit card are not protected by this rule unless payment by check or money order is sent immediately following the order.

If you have a complaint about a product or service, write a letter stating your complaint and include photocopies of all related information, such as previous letters and cancelled checks. Do not send original documents. Ask for a response within 30 days. If you do not receive a response, you can contact the Better Business Bureau, the Direct Mail Association, or the Federal Trade Commission.

The companies included here are among the most reputable in New England. They are deservedly proud of their products and their heritage. Many were started because the founder wanted to share a new discovery or the passion for a product with neighbors and friends. Now it's time to share that with the rest of the country.

NEW ENGLAND

BY MAIL

Eat, DRINK, AND BE MERRY

THE FOOD SPECIALTIES
OF NEW ENGLAND

Applecrest Farm Orchards, Inc.

Route 88
Hampton Falls, New Hampshire 03844
(603) 926-3721

Remember those cool, New England fall days and the crispy crunch of a just-picked apple? Applecrest Farm Orchards can help you bring those memories back for friends or relatives by sending them a bit of New England.

One of the oldest and largest apple orchards in New England, Applecrest ships the largest and most perfect apples almost as soon as they are picked. For more than 75 years Applecrest has been shipping several varieties of apples, maple syrup, their famous white cheddar cheese, homemade fruit pies, several honeys and preserves, and special gift packs. They provide their customers with delicious treats and delightful memories of home.

Prices start at $14.50 for one pint of pure maple syrup. A one-layer pack of 18 apples is $17.50, and a three-pound wheel of cheese is $18.00. Prices do include shipping and will vary according to shipping distance.

Free catalog. Wholesale available. Price quotes by phone or letter. Products guaranteed. Goods are packed to order. Shipped within one week by UPS, U.S. mail, or Federal Express with instructions: Perishable—protect from extreme heat and cold. Payment by MasterCard, Visa, check, or money order.

Retail stores

Apple Mart	Big Apple	Apple Cart
Route 88	Route 1	Junction 150 & 110
Hampton Falls, NH	Hampton Falls, NH	Amesbury, MA
(603) 926-3721	(603) 926-8358	(508) 388-0405
Daily	Daily	Daily
8:00 A.M. to 6:00 P.M.	8:00 A.M. to 8:00 P.M.	8:00 A.M. to 7:00 P.M.

Bacon's Sugar House

Dublin Road
Jaffrey Center, New Hampshire 03454
(603) 532-8836

The Bacons are proud of their heritage as producers of high quality maple syrup. The Dublin Road Sugar Orchard has been producing maple syrup since 1780. The present sugar house has been in operation since 1910. They still have a bottle of that 1910 syrup, an example of the pride they have in every bottle of maple syrup they sell.

The Bacons tap the trees, some of which are more than 200 years old, in late February, needing 40 gallons of sap to make one gallon of syrup. They boil down the sap and package the syrup in unbreakable plastic jugs Charles Bacon designed to look like old-fashioned earthenware jugs and flasks. They specialize in Christmas selections, and will ship maple syrup and sugar to you or to friends and relatives who miss the flavor of a warm New England breakfast.

Retail shop at the farm, open daily most of the year. Call for hours.

Free catalog. Wholesale available. Price quotes by letter or phone. Prices include shipping. Goods are stocked, guaranteed, and shipped by UPS or U.S. mail the day after order received. Payment by check or money order.

Bacon's Sugar House

E.D. de B.

	Shipped East of the Mississippi	Shipped West of the Mississippi
Half Pint	$8.35	$8.85
14-ounce Maple Leaf Flask	10.60	11.10
16.9-ounce Log Cabin	13.80	14.55
Pint	11.35	11.85
Quart	17.75	18.70
Half Gallon	28.15	29.60
Gallon	47.50	50.20

Bear Meadow Farm

Rt. 2, Moore Road
Florida, Massachusetts 01247
(413) 663-9241

For more than fifteen years, Bear Meadow Farm has been producing condiments, herbs, and perennial plants of uncommon quality.

All the selections were painstakingly developed at this family-owned business, from the Bear Bite Mustard, Rhubarb Chutney, Hot Pepper, Thyme, and Sage Jellies to the herbed vinegars that are exclusive to the Bear Meadow kitchens.

They also offer a wide selection of special items such as apple or cranberry catsup, honey mint sauce, monk's mustard, and spiced wild blueberries. In addition to their herbed vinegars, they offer three fruit vinegars—cranberry, blueberry, and raspberry.

Since their goal is to provide only the purest foods, their jellies, preserves, and relishes are made with a minimum of other ingredients added to the fruits, herbs, and vegetables.

Prices ranges from $2.50 for 13.2 ounces of basil vinegar to $4.15 for 10 ounces of apple chutney. All herb jellies, and fruit jams, preserves, and jellies are $3.95 for 10 ounces. Mustards and other specialties are $4.15 for 10 ounces. Prices do not include shipping, but there is a 10 percent discount for orders of a dozen or more of any one item.

Call or write for more information. Shipped by UPS inside the continental United States (U.S. mail by request). Will ship to Canada. Payment by check.

Jams and Preserves	*Special Things*	*Relishes, Catsups and Sauces*
Black Cherry Preserve	Apple Butter	Beet Relish
Strawberry Rhubarb Jam	Brandied Cherries	Corn Relish
Red Raspberry Preserve	Brandied Peaches	Apple Catsup
Red and Black Raspberry Jam	Spiced Wild Blueberries	Cranberry Catsup
Bramble Preserve Strawberry Preserve	Hot Pepper Jelly	Honey Mint Sauce
Wild Blueberry Preserve	*Mustards*	Old Fashioned Barbecue Sauce
Special Peach Jam	Honey-Herb	Tomato-Olive Pasta Sauce
Fruit Jellies	Horseradish	*Herb Vinegars*
Cranberry	Monk's	Basil
Grape	Bear-Bite	Dill
Apple	*Chutneys*	Garlic-Wine
Cranberry-Wine	Cranberry	Mint
Herb Jellies	Apple	Tarragon-Wine
Rose Geranium	Rhubarb	Thyme
Garden Mint	*Fruit Vinegars*	#1-Savory, Marjoram, Chives, Thyme
Thyme	Cranberry	#2-Basil, Rosemary, Tarragon, Bay
Rosemary	Blueberry	#3-Garlic-Herb
Sage	Raspberry	
Tarragon		

Brewster River Mill

Mill Street
Jeffersonville, Vermont 05464
(802) 644-2987

In the early 1970s the Albright family discovered a Vermont treasure: the historic Brewster River Mill which has overlooked its clear mountain stream since the 1700s. Since 1976 the Albrights have worked to restore this landmark, taking great pains to do the work in the traditional way; like using cut nails and wooden pegs to join the timbers. Although the mill is currently Vermont's only steam-powered gristmill, the Albrights hope some day to return the mill to water power.

To help pay for the restoration, the Albrights operate the mill and offer their customers products that reflect the same dedication to quality that they have shown in restoring the mill. Everything they offer is made locally and contains natural ingredients. The grains are organically grown; most of the maple syrup comes from the family's sugarplace. The other products have to meet the Albrights' stringent quality guidelines. Their specialty products include jams, jellies, preserves, and marmalades—all of them delicious and all-natural.

Visitors to the mill also have more waiting for them than excellent food. They can watch the grain being ground into flour, walk to the Scott Covered Bridge (c. 1890) 150 yards away, relax on the rocks overlooking the river, or just browse in the gift shop. Visit Brewster River Mill sometime for a pleasant afternoon trip back into the past.

Free catalog. Wholesale available. Price quotes by letter and phone. Prices do not include shipping. Product guaranteed. Goods stocked, shipped by U.S. mail or UPS within two weeks. Payment by Master-Card, Visa, check, or money order.

Stoneground Flour and Meal	
Whole wheat flour (6 lbs.)	$2.75
Hi-gluten white flour (6 lbs.)	2.75
Oat flour (3 lbs.)	2.50
Rye flour (3 lbs.)	1.35
Rolled oats (3 lbs.)	1.50
Cornmeal (3 lbs.)	1.50
Oat bran (2 lbs.)	1.95
Cracked wheat (3 lbs.)	1.25
Buckwheat flour (3 lbs.)	2.75

Kenyon Mixes	
4-grain pancake	$2.95
Corn bread and muffin	3.45
Buttermilk/Honey pancake	3.45
Honey/Buckwheat pancake	3.45
Breakfast Box	8.50

Maple Syrup	
Gallon	$45.00
Half gallon	24.95
Quart	14.95
Pint	8.95
Half pint	5.50
Cabin can (16.9 oz.)	10.95
Maple sugar (8 oz.)	4.95
Maple butter (8 oz.)	4.95
Maple candy (3.75 oz.)	4.50

Miscellaneous	
Vermont common crackers	$10.95
Hot chocolate mix	1.95
Roast sweet corn	2.99/lb.

Jams, Jellies	
All flavors	$3.95
Strawberry *Blackberry	
Strawberry-Rhubarb	
Blueberry*Raspberry*Cranberry-Apple	
Red Raspberry Marmalade*Rhubarb	
Pumpkin Marmalade*Cider Jelly	
Cranberry Marmalade	
Spiced Apple Butter	
Raspberry Apple Butter	

Brown Bag Cookie Art

A Hill Design Company
Box F
Hill, New Hampshire 03243
(800) 228-4488 (credit card orders only)
(603) 934-2650

While wandering around in Boston's Chinatown one day, Lucy Ross Natkiel saw in the window of a small grocery store a tray of almond cookies that had been formed into enchanting shapes—carp, lions, Buddhas—with every detail perfectly formed.

She had never seen anything like it, and she realized that there was more to baking cookies than she had thought. Instead of the ordinary rolled, drop, and bar cookies most people think of, why not exquisite molded cookies? Brown Bag Cookie Art was born.

What was new to Lucy is actually an old art. The Chinese have been making molded cookies for centuries. Carved molds have also been used in Europe for hundreds of years. Cookie molds probably came to America in the eighteenth century and are still very much a part of our everyday lives. Although most people don't think about it, some of America's favorite cookies carry a molded imprint.

Although Brown Bag Cookie Art specializes in the ceramic molds for cookies, they also carry molds for shortbread. Lucy has even compiled a cookie recipe book with hints on baking molded cookies. They carry more than 30 molds in everyday shapes, such as a teddy bear or a cat holding a bouquet of flowers, Christmas designs, and molds for everybody's favorite dinosaurs. Cookie molds are $12.00; shortbread molds are $23.00.

Free catalog. Wholesale available. Goods stocked and shipped UPS. Payment by MasterCard, Visa, check, or money order.

Cookie Molds	Goose	Mrs. Cat	Stegosaurus
Beautiful Swan	Rocking Horse	Saint Nicholas	Triceratops
Cat With Flowers	Gingerbread House	Toy Train	Tyrannosaurus Rex
Teddy Bear	Clown Doll	Toy Boat	
Elaine's Cow	Girl Doll	Angel With Lute	*Shortbread Molds*
Wooly Lamb	Boy Doll	Angel With Heart	Flowers and Berries
Duck Family	Victorian Heart	Christmas Tree	Swans
Big Chicken	Folk Heart	Christmas Stocking	Wildflowers
Big Fat Pig	Quilted Heart	Christmas Star	
Big Bunny	Mr. Rabbit	Holly Wreath	

Cherry Hill Cannery

MR 1
Barre Vermont 05641
(802) 479-2558

In the heart of Vermont, a small farm company produces a line of gourmet foods from organically grown vegetables and alar-free apples. Specializing in sauces, jellies and preserves, the Cherry Hill Cannery chefs draw recipes and experiences from all over the world to perfect their Vermont products.

Miguel's Salsa is from a recipe that Mike Henzel brought back from the southwest United States and made locally famous in his Stowe, Vermont, restaurant, the Stowe-away. Dell'amore's Marinara Sauce is the recipe that Frank Dell'amore's grandmother Filomena gave him. Annie's Farmhouse Foods are a line of sauces, mustards, and vinaigrettes that Annie learned to make as a gourmet chef in New York.

Some of their favorite recipes, however, were created in Vermont: the Panhandler Conserves of Stowe's Patty Girourd, Uncle's Dave's Ketchup and Bloody Mary Fixin's. And, of course, Dugout Dan's Secret Sauce and Teriyaki Marinade, made famous by Dan's Dugout restaurant that he carved into the side of a Vermont hill in hopes of curing his rheumatism.

The gift boxes or individual items are enough to make you walk lighter and smile wider.

Prices range from $2.29 for 16 ounces of Unsweetened Applesauce to $14.29 for 32 ounces of Fancy Maple Syrup. Gift boxes start at $16.49.

You can also buy all their products at the Cherry Hill Retail Store on Barre-Montpelier Road, Rt. 302, in Barre. Call for hours.

Free catalog. Wholesale available. Price quotes by phone. Products stocked and guaranteed. Shipped by UPS within two weeks. Will ship to Canada. Payment by MasterCard, Visa, check, or money order.

Concord Teacakes, Etc., Inc.

P. O. Box 134
Concord, Massachusetts 01742
(508) 369-7644

In 1984 Judy Fersch took Emily Dickinson's original recipe for a Brandy Raisincake and began making a few cakes for shops in the Concord area. Then Marian Burros tasted one at the New York Food and Beverage Show and wrote a short paragraph about the cake in her *New York Times* "De Gustibus" column, saying "It will make fruitcake fanciers of those who shudder at the sight of one." Ten days later, Judy's phone was ringing off the hook, and she was in the mail order business.

All of Judy's cakes and teacakes are available year-round, but the Christmas season calls for her to start her holiday baking in June. By December she will have used more than four thousand eggs and one million raisins. Not bad for a woman who started baking 20 cakes a week in an Elks Club kitchen.

In addition to Emily Dickinson's Brandy Raisin-cake, Judy also makes Almond Lemon Cake, Chocolate Chocolate Cake, and a selection of teacakes, those wonderful fine-grained quick breads—not too sweet or too fancy—that go perfectly with tea.

The Brandy Raisincakes come in two sizes: a 12-ounce loaf for $14.00 and a 24-ounce loaf for $21.00. The Almond Lemon and Chocolate Chocolate 8-inch bundt cakes are $16.00 each. The teacakes come in Cinnamon Pecan Apple, Almond Lemon, and Dark Gingerbread flavors and are also available in 8-inch bundts for $11.50 each. Mini-bundts are $2.25, loaf cakes $3.75.

Judy's retail store, at 50 Beharrel St. in Concord, is only open on Friday from 7:00 A.M. to 2:00 P.M. and Saturday from 9:00 A.M. to 12:00 P.M.

Free catalog. Wholesale available. Price quotes available by letter or phone. Goods stocked, with some made to order. Shipped by UPS. Payment by check or money order.

Coski's Choice, Inc.

P. O. Box 544
Bellows Falls, Vermont 05101
(802) 463-4561

All-natural, nutritious food is essential for good health and a long life. We have known that for a long time. Now it's time to share that with our best friends: our pets.

Coski's Choice offers a full line of hand-made treats for family pets. Each cookie and bone is made by hand with tender loving care from the finest ingredients. They contain no added salt, sugar, additives, artificial coloring, or preservatives. Coski's will even prepare custom foods for the pet with special dietary needs.

They think that your pet will agree this wholesome indulgence is "The Right Bite!"

Large Bones (8½ inches) are $1.75 each. Medium Bones (4 inches) are $.70 each. Beef, chicken, cheese, or health cookies are $.40 each or $4.50 per dozen. Gift packs start at $6.50 for two dozen assorted cookies. Cookie flavors and shapes include Beef Bunnies, Chicken Chickens, Ham Hogs, Cheese Quackers, Tuna Fish, Small Liver Chip Cookies, Liver Paté Hydrants, Veggie Acorns, Carrot Cars, Peanut Butter Stars, Chocolate Babies, Apple Cinnamon Hearts, and Banana Spice Bears.

Coski's Choice has a retail shop on Imtec Lane in the Bellows Falls, Vermont Industrial Park, open Monday through Friday from 9:00 A.M. to 5:00 P.M.

Free catalog. Wholesale available. Price quotes by letter or phone for special orders only. Minimum order of $10.00. Products are made and packaged to order. Shipped by UPS or motor freight within three weeks. Packages marked "Fragile." Will ship to Canada. Payment by C.O.D., check, or money order.

Craigston Cheese Company

Box 267, 45 Dodge's Row
Wenham, Massachusetts 01984
(508) 468-7497
(800) 365-6299

In 1976, when Tim and Susan Hollander began a dairy farm on 15 acres in Wenham, they were determined to provide fresh food for their family. The dairy farm prospered, but milk production could not support the family. They didn't want to get rid of the herd, so they had to find a way to pay for it. The answer was to make cheese, but not just any cheese.

Camembert, a mold-ripened soft cheese with a distinctive aroma, is one of the trickiest cheeses to make. The slightest change in humidity or temperature will destroy a batch. Since it is one of the French cheeses that does not import well, the Hollanders had a good opportunity for supplying the demand in America. However, making Camembert in Massachusetts was no simple matter. The Hollanders sent their 15-year-old son to Normandy one summer to work on French cheese farms; they imported the molds, vats, curing knives, and storage racks from Germany; they bought wrapping foil from France; and took a cheese-making course at the University of Guelph in Ontario.

After five years of research and preparation the Hollanders began marketing their Camembert cheese. "Customers went wild," said Jan Marcaurelle, the cheese connoisseur of Bruni's Market in Ipswich, Massachusetts. The *New York Times* reported, "This sumptuously creamy cheese stands up to any French Camembert." It "ranks among the best we've tasted," reported *Food and Wine*. Julia Child has suggested that the Hollanders should export Craigston Camembert to France. And the America Cheese Society has awarded Craigston Camembert two blue ribbons.

An 8-ounce round is $9.95, including shipping. Additional cheeses are $5.95 each.

Sold in more than 650 markets in 46 states, Craigston Camembert is a true example of American excellence.

Call or write for more information. Wholesale is available. Price quotes by letter or phone. Goods are stocked and shipped UPS within one week. Will ship to Canada. Payment by check only.

Crosswoods Vineyards

75 Chester Maine Road
North Stonington, Connecticut 06359
(203) 535-2205

Perched on a plateau overlooking the Atlantic Ocean, Crosswoods Winery is situated in a location as beautiful and pleasant as it is practical. The climate, absolutely perfect for producing the finest wine grapes, is as important to the success of Crosswoods as any part of the modern, efficient 20,000- gallon winery.

Planning for Crosswood began in 1975. After a massive amount of research into soils, climates, grape varieties, equipment, and winemaking, the first grapes were planted in the spring of 1981. Today, Crosswoods is devoted to the production of quality wines made from classic vinifera grapes such as Chardonnay, Pinot Noir, Gamay Noir, Riesling, and Gewurz-traminer.

Housed in the shells of nineteenth-century dairy barns, Crosswoods is operated by Susan and Hugh Connell, their three sons and a dedicated staff. Much effort went into earning a reputation for making premium wines, and the Connells and their staff are dedicated to maintaining that reputation.

Praise earned by their 1985 Merlot resulted in an agreement to export Crosswoods wines to France. Both *The Wine Advocate*'s Robert Parker, and *Nightfall*'s James S. Nicas recognized the 1985 Merlot as one of America's best wines of that vintage. That 1985 Merlot is now sold out, but Crosswoods continues to produce wines unsurpassed in quality and recognition.

Wines are sold at the winery, and customers are welcome to tour its historic setting. Free brochure. Wholesale available. Wines shipped UPS, delivery limited to the state of Connecticut. Call for prices of available wines. Payment by MasterCard or Visa.

Fiddler's Green Farm

RFD 1, Box 656N
Belfast, Maine 04915
(207) 338-3568

Demonstrating food at markets and fairs is very risky. A lot is given to people who grab and walk away never to be seen again. It takes a very special product to stop people in their tracks, and make them turn around and come back to say, "This is great! What is it?"

"It" is Penobscot Porridge. Or Irish Soda Bread. Or Buttermilk Spice Cake. Or any of the other foods prepared from Fiddler's Green's organically grown and milled food mixes.

It takes a very special product to stop people in their tracks, make them . . . say, "This is great! What is it?"

In 1974 David Kennedy, a ship's pilot, started Fiddler's Green with the dream of growing food in the purest, most natural way. He used no chemicals of any kind on the soil on the plants, or during the milling of the grains. When Captain Kennedy was killed in 1985, the farm was sold to Nancy Galland and Richard Stander who have carried on Captain Kennedy's dream, expanded the farm's production capabilities, and added a number of products to their organic mix product line.

The results have been a rousing success. The number of orders increase daily, and the organic mixes have received rave reviews in *The New York Times*, *Changing Times*, the *Boston Globe*, the *Washington Post, Cook's Magazine*, and *The Chicago Tribune*.

Penobscot Porridge, one of the most popular products, is a blend of wheat, rye, corn, and brown rice, resulting in a hot breakfast cereal with a nutty flavor that is grainy, not mushy like oatmeal.

Their Bread and Biscuit Mix also contains an authentic recipe for Irish Soda Bread that slices like yeast bread and makes great toast. The Toasted Buckwheat and Buttermilk Pancake and Muffin Mix produces light pancakes and muffins. Top the pancakes with Fiddler's Green syrups or jams. They also offer *certified* organically grown coffees to add the finishing touch to an all-natural breakfast.

They have also introduced two wheat-free products, Oats 'n Barley Pancake Mix, and Oat Bran and Brown Rice Hot Cereal.

Individual mixes, gift packs, and gift items such as T-shirts and aprons may be ordered. Gift packs start at $8.95; mixes start at $2.64 for 1½ pounds.

Free catalog. Wholesale available. Price quotes by letter or phone. Goods stocked and shipped by UPS, U.S. mail, or common carrier within two weeks. Payment by MasterCard, Visa, check, or money order.

Graffam Bros.

P. O. Box 340T
Rockport, Maine 04856
(800) 535-5358 (outside Maine)
(207) 236-3396 (inside Maine)

Since 1946, Graffam Bros. has been offering a unique service to lobster-lovers all over the country. They will ship live Maine lobsters to your door, ensuring that your lobster dinner will be as fresh as possible.

The lobsters that Graffam Bros. ship are trapped by independent Maine fishermen who work even through the challenging winters. After the lobsters are delivered to Graffam Bros. in Rockport, they are kept in special refrigerated hold tanks in the same fresh saltwater environment in which they were caught.

When you place your order, the lobsters are carefully chosen, following your instructions. Then they are packed, along with fresh seaweed and "cold packs," into insulated, leak-proof containers and shipped by overnight express directly to your door. Thanks to Graffam Bros. you can enjoy the taste of Maine no matter where you are.

Prices for the lobsters range from $53.00 for two one-pound lobsters to $362.00 for 20 two-pound lobsters. Prices include all shipping charges.

If you want to add to that "taste of Maine," Graffam Bros. also ships clams by the peck or bushel at $4.00 per pound.

Their retail store is at **Rear 18 Central Street** in Rockport. They are open Monday through Friday from 7:00 A.M. to 2:30 P.M. and Saturday from 8:00 A.M. to 10:00 A.M.

---

*You get to enjoy
the taste of Maine
no matter where you are.*

Free brochure and price list. Wholesale available. Gift certificates can be ordered for use at a later date. Products guaranteed. Shipped Federal Express overnight. Will ship to Canada. Payment by MasterCard, Visa, check, or money order.

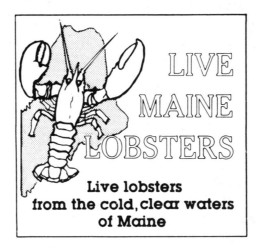

Live lobsters
from the cold, clear waters
of Maine

Grafton Village Apple Company

RR 3
Box 236 D
Grafton, Vermont 05146-8905
(800) 843-4822
(802) 843-2406

A roadside fruit stand is a familiar sight along rural highways. Most people who start those stands, however, do not expect it to turn into a thriving mail order business with more than 15,000 satisfied and loyal customers.

Janice and Joe Pollio's business was once a small fruit stand just like hundreds of others. But their customers kept returning, and began to ask Joe and Janice if they would send their farm's products to Aunt Sue and Cousin Fred. Soon the stand was a minor part of their business. Their mail order business is now their primary concern.

In addition to apple gift boxes, the Grafton Apple Company offers the pride of Vermont products with a line that ranges from maple products, pancake mixes, and fruitcakes to carefully aged cheeses, maple-sweetened jams and jellies, salad dressings, vinegars, and smoked meats. Gift packs start at $19.95.

Many of these items are also available at their retail store, which is on Route 121 in Grafton. Call for hours.

Free catalog. Wholesale available. Price quotes by phone. Products guaranteed. Goods stocked and shipped within two weeks by UPS. Will ship to Canada. Payment by American Express, MasterCard, Visa, check, or money order.

Pure Maple Syrup	8 ounces	$ 5.95
	128 ounces	58.95
The Vermont Maple House	16.9 ounces	11.95
Vermont All-Natural Fruitcake	2.5 pounds	23.95
Vermont Apple Gift Box	16 apples	14.95
Aged Vermont Cheddar Cheese	8 ounces	3.95
Grafton Goodjams with Maple Syrup	12 ounces	8.95
Cob-smoked Boneless Ham	7-8 pounds	75.95

Green Briar Jam Kitchen

6 Discovery Hill Road
East Sandwich, Massachusetts 02537
(508) 888-6870

Operated by the Thornton W. Burgess Society, Green Briar Jam Kitchen has been producing New England's favorite jellies and preserves since 1903.

Still made in small batches in a turn-of-the-century kitchen, Green Briar's products include more than

"'Tis a wonderful thing to sweeten the world which is in a jam and needs preserving."
—Thornton W. Burgess

sixty flavors of jams, jellies, and marmalades, as well as sun-cooked fruits, cranberry products, pickles and relishes, and specialty items such as Mae's Mincemeat, Plum and Rhubarb Conserves, and Red or Yellow Tomato with Ginger.

All jars are six ounces and prices range from $3.00 for Bread and Butter pickles to $4.25 for the sun-cooked fruits. Gift packs are available, including a Cranberry Medley, the ideal Cape Cod gift.

Retail shop on site. They are open Monday through Saturday from 10:00 A.M. to 4:00 P.M. and on Sunday from 1:00 PM. to 4:00 P.M.

Free catalog. Goods are stocked and shipped within four weeks by UPS. Will ship to Canada. Payment by MasterCard, Visa, or check.

Jams	*Cranberry Products*	*Pickles and Relishes*	*Specialty Items*
Apricot	Currant	Lime	Nectarines with Brandy
Blueberry	Mint	Orange	Peaches with Brandy
Ginger Rhubarb	Paradise		Plums with Rum
Nectarine	Quince	*Pickles and Relishes*	Strawberries
Peach		Bread and Butter	Strawberries with Vodka
Plum	*Cranberry Products*	Frankline Special	
Plum Rum	Cranberry Conserve	Martha's Mustard	*Specialty Items*
Raspberry	Cranberry Chutney	Melon Rind Pickes	Beach Plum Jelly
Strawberry	Cranberry Orange Pineapple	Piccalilli	Apple Chutney
Strawberry Rhubarb	Jellied Cranberry Sauce	Pottsfield Pickle	Mae's Mincemeat
	Whole Cranberry Sauce	Pumpkin Pickle	Orange Pineapple
Jellies		Chili Sauce	Pear Butter
Apple	*Marmalades*	Hot Pepper Relish	Pineapple Mint
Apple Rum	Carrot	Ripe Tomato Relish	Plum Conserve
Cinnamon	Ginger Orange	Sweet Pepper Relish	Rhubarb Conserve
Crabapple	Grapefruit		Red Tomato with Ginger
Cranberry Apple	Grapefruit with Cherries	*Sun-Cooked Fruits*	Yellow Tomato With Ginger
Concord Grape	Lemon	Apricot with Brandy	
	Lemon-Lime	Blueberries with Kirsch	

Harman's Cheese and Country Store

P. O. Box H624
Route 117
Sugar Hill, New Hampshire 03585
(603) 823-8000

Harman's boasts "The World's Greatest" cheddar cheese, but the specialty of the house is the personalized service offered to each customer. According to Maxine, she would "rather you call or stop in for a chat." She's there seven days a week during the summer and six days a week during the winter.

Besides the cheese, they offer hard-to-find, pure, top quality gourmet delicacies like kippers, crab meat, soldier beans, New Hampshire products, and New England common crackers, salad dressings, jams, and other unique specialties.

Maxine is ready and eager to discuss any of their products, from the cheese and maple syrup to the smoked meats and crackers, from the herb mixes and preserves to the candy and the store-made cheese spreads. She's ready to share the wealth of the old store with you or your friends, relatives, or business acquaintances. All you have to do is ask.

Free catalog. Products guaranteed. Goods are stocked and shipped within two weeks, with most orders shipped the same day. Will ship to Canada. Payment by check or money order.

Cheddar Cheese	1 pound	$5.25
Crab Meat	6.5-ounce tin	4.85
She-Crab Soup	10.5-ounce can	2.00
Smoke Salmon	3.75-ounce tin	2.40
Pure Maple Syrup	1 pint	8.50
Maple Butter	16-ounce jar	9.00
Maple Sugar	2.5-ounce jar	3.70
Maple Candy	5.5-ounce box	5.95
Dickinson Preserves	12-ounce jar	3.50
Hero Preserves	12-ounce jar	3.75
Allberry Fruit Farm Jame	5-ounce jar	3.00
Tas-tee Salad Dressing	16-ounce bottle	3.85
Sweet/Sour Salad Dressing	8-ounce bottle	2.40
Old-Fashioned Stick Candy	6-stick bundle	1.00
Licorice Laces	3.75-ounce bag	1.30
Rock Candy	5-ounce bag	2.00
New England Chunky Ketchup	12-ounce bottle	3.50

The Herb Garden

Kinnebrook Road
Dept. R
Worthington, Massachusetts 01098
(413) 238-5355

The wine herbal vinegars of The HerbGarden have an unsurpassed quality and flavor that keep their customers coming back for more. Made with fresh herbs and locally grown berries, the six traditional flavors of The Herb Garden vinegars are handmade in small batches.

The Herb Garden also offers a non-traditional sweet and sour Maple-Raspberry flavor vinegar with a hint of basil combined with maple syrup and raspberry vinegar. Customers report that this oil-free dressing tastes great on French fries, baked chicken, and filet mignon. It is also a delightful topping for salads.

Although herbal vinegars are their trademark, The Herb Garden also offers Indian sugar and pure maple syrup.

Five-ounce bottles of the vinegars are $2.95, a six-pack is $14.00. The 12.7-ounce bottles are $4.20. The Maple-Raspberry vinegar is a bit more expensive at $3.00 for a five-ounce bottle.

Free catalog for SASE. Wholesale available. Products stocked and guaranteed, shipped by UPS within four to five weeks. Payment by check or money order.

Herbal Vinegars

Chive Flower
A pale pink vinegar made with the chive blossom.
It's great on steamed vegetables.

Garlic-Dill
Terrific mixed with oil or used alone on chicken,
new potatoes, or in marinade recipes.

Opal Basil
Made with the deep purple-leaf basil which has a slightly
spicier taste than green basil. Great on tomatoes and salads,
and as an ingredient in vinaigrettes.

Raspberry
Good on salad and with chicken, but really shines
when used with sugar on fresh fruit.

Tarragon
Perhaps the best known herbal vinegar,
it is especially good on fish or scrambled eggs.

Thyme
Best in game and wild fowl marinades, but is also
good in German potato salad or sprinkled over potato chips.

Hopkins Vineyards

Hopkins Road
New Preston, Connecticut 06777
(203) 868-7954

Among the rolling hills of western Connecticut are historic villages, beautiful scenery, and a special treasure: The Hopkins Vineyard. The 20 acres of vineyard produce six types of grapes for the award-winning wines, which have won more medals than any other northeastern winery and received 13 gold medals in just three years!

The Hopkins family has worked this land for more than 200 years, and the care each generation took with the crops and the soil has resulted in a fertile area for their cherished vineyard. The family believes this makes a difference: "Special wines from a special place."

Seyval Blanc
Subtle and well balanced, the driest of their whites.
Waramaug White
Made from Aurora grapes, dry with a clean finish.
Barn Red
Blended from Marechal Foch
and a touch of Leon Millot grapes.
Sachem's Picnic
Light, semi-sweet red.
First Blush
Fruity and semi-sweet, made from Cayuga White
and a touch of Marechal Foch.
Yankee Cider
Hard cider made from locally grown apples.
Vignoles Sauternes
A honeyed sweet Chardonnay cross.
Their greatest award winner.

Wines can be ordered by the bottle or the case, and cases can be mixed. Prices start at approximately $6.00 per bottle. Mail order is available only in the state of Connecticut. The retail store at the Vineyard is open daily May to January from 10:00 A.M. to 5:00 P.M.; during January to April they are open Friday, Saturday, and Sunday from 10:00 A.M. to 5:00 P.M.

Free catalog. Wholesale available to any establishment with a liquor license. Products shipped UPS within one week. Payment by MasterCard, Visa, or check.

Maine's Own Treats

Bar Harbor Road
RR #1, Box 16A
Ellsworth, Maine 04605
(207) 667-8888

In 1979, a small home kitchen in Blue Hill, Maine, was the birthplace of a unique operation. Using as many native ingredients as possible—and no preservatives or dyes—handmade jellies, jams, and syrups were made in small batches and sold under the label of Maine's Own Treats.

As word of the quality and fine taste of Maine's Own Treats grew, so did the business. The company finally moved to a small community on the edge of Acadia National Park. Keeping in mind that homemade quality is what made the company a success, Maine's Own Treats are still made on an average kitchen stove in small batches.

Maine's Own Treats wants each jar of jam to carry the finest quality and flavor possible, so that when you open a jar some crisp fall morning and spread that jam on a piece of toast, you'll experience Maine one more time.

Maine's Own Treats features 25 flavors of jams and five flavors of syrup. Sold by single jars, cases of 12, or in gift packs. Prices start at $2.00 for jars, $22.00 for cases, and $5.00 for gift packs.

Their retail store, on Route 3 between Ellsworth and Bar Harbor, specializes in Maine food products. They are open daily from June to December from 8:00 A.M. to 6:00 P.M.; from January to May from 9:00 A.M. to 4:00 P.M.

Keeping in mind that homemade quality is what made the company a success, Maine's Own Treats are still made on an average kitchen stove in small batches.

Free catalog. Wholesale available. Minimum order $10.00. Products guaranteed. Goods are stocked; large orders or special packaging made to order. Goods shipped UPS. Limited shipping to Canada. Payment by American Express, MasterCard, Visa, check, or money order.

Jam Flavors			*Syrup Flavors*
Blueberry Jam	Raspberry Apple Jam	Punch Bowl Jam (10 fruits)	Blueberry
Yummy Toast Spread	Citrus Jubille Marmalade	Choke Cherry Jam	Strawberry
Strawberry Rhubarb Jam	Rosehip Jam	Zucchini-Pineapple-	Red Raspberry
Raspberry Rhubarb Jam	Peach Jam	Ginger Marmalade	Black Raspberry
Wild Blackberry Jam	Pear Preserve	Boysenberry Jam	100% Pure Maple
Strawberry Pineapple Jam	Cherry Jam	Blueberry Rhubarb Jam	
Strawberry Apple Jam	Black Raspberry Jam	High Bush Cranberry Jam	
Raspberry Peach Jam	Plum Jam	Grape Apple Jelly	
	Apricot Pineapple Jam		

MAINE'S OWN TREATS
Famous Jams & Jellies

Maple Grove Farms

167 Portland Street
St. Johnsbury, Vermont 05819
(802) 748-5141

Imagine a country kitchen filled with the delicious and welcoming aroma of sizzling smoked bacon, buttermilk pancakes, and pure, sweet maple syrup. All you need to make the morning complete would be the presence of your family and friends to enjoy this warm hearty breakfast.

You gather the people, and Maple Grove Farms will provide the breakfast; but bacon, pancakes, and syrup are only the beginning.

Since 1915, Maple Grove has been known for the quality of their pure maple syrup, Vermont cheeses, and smoked meats. Their maple syrup is available in all grades, and comes in a variety of containers, from a log cabin tin to Currier and Ives stoneware jugs. Other maple products include maple cream, honey maple butter, maple sugar, and maple candy.

To go along with their maple candy, they make blueberry, cranberry, and peppermint candies, and dark and white chocolate cows which they sell in pairs or herds.

Their Vermont Aged Cheddar Cheese is made from fresh whole milk from nearby farms that has been curdled, compressed, and aged in the same time-honored way as generations of Vermont cheesemakers. You can buy it in a three-pound wheel, or in one of their gift packs. They also carry the cheddar cheese flavored with bits of sage, and cheese that has been smoked with hickory or maple.

They use maple as well as corn cobs to smoke their meats, then cure them with maple sugar and spices, leaving a sweet, smoky flavor. Fully cooked, these are ready for your table. Try their sprial cut ham or a whole turkey. If you need a smaller portion, try their smoked ham and cheese gift pack or a smoked pheasant or duck. They also carry Canadian bacon, sockeye salmon, and a smoked slab bacon.

Top off your breakfast with their fruit preserves or syrups. Or try the Old English Plum Pudding for a treat.

They also carry relishes, dressings, and a variety of gift packs. The list seems to go on forever. Breakfast is just the beginning—they can make your whole day delicious.

Free catalog. Products guaranteed. Goods are stocked and shipped by UPS unless otherwise requested. Payment by American Express, MasterCard, Visa, check, or money order.

Pure Dark Amber Maple Syrup	1 pint	$11.95	Smoked Turkey Breast	6-7 pounds	$29.90
Maple Cream	1-pound jar	13.95	Smoked Sockeye Salmon Filet	1.125 pounds	39.50
Maple Candy	3-pound box	19.95	Brace of Pheasant	4-5 pounds	54.95
Aged Cheddar Cheese	3-pound wheel	19.95	Old English Plum Pudding	14 ounces	18.50
Irish Whiskey Cake	2.5 pounds	27.75	Popcorn Trio	2-gallon tin	17.95
Vermont Velvet Cheesecake	1.5 pounds	15.95	Homemade Fudge	1.5 pound tin	12.50

McMillen's Gourmet Foods

P. O. Box 63
Eliot, Maine 03903
(207) 439-2481

In 1981, sharing a love of gardening and cooking, newlyweds Debbie McMillen and Jon Cavallo began experimenting with some of their "old family recipes." When the results started winning awards, Debbie and Jon expanded their business, but not their operation. All of their specialty foods are still made in small batches in the kitchen of their home, but now they have to make a lot more of those batches to keep up with the demand for their extensive line of sauces, jellies, jams, conserves, and seasonings.

Their first award winners were Debbie's Garden Relish and Jalapeño Jelly. These have been joined by their best seller, Champagne Mustard Sauce, and other delectables such as Cranberry Banana Jam and Strawberry Rhubarb Preserves.

They have also introduced a line of Midlife Crisis Spices, five delightful packages that come with several suggested recipes. The spices are available for $2.50 per three-ounce package or $12.00 for five packages.

If you've looked over their list and still aren't sure what to try, start with their Sampler Gift Box, which holds 3-ounce jars each of Champagne Mustard Sauce, Sultan's Sauce, Jalapeño Jelly, and two Breakfast Jams. They also have two different gift baskets made to your requests.

All McMillen jarred products are salt-free. A three-ounce jar is $2.99, a 5.25-ounce jar is $4.50, and a 12-ounce jar is $6.50.

McMillen's Gourmet Foods are available through the gourmet and specialty shops as well as through mail order. Send a SASE for information. Wholesale is available. Products guaranteed. Goods are stocked and shipped by UPS within three weeks. Payment by check only.

New England Maple Museum

P. O. Box 1615
Rutland, Vermont 05701
(802) 483-9414

Maple syrup is America's oldest and one of the most well-known agricultural products. Until 1977, it was also one of the most misunderstood. Knowledge of the maple industry was not widely known before Dona and Tom Olson opened the New England Maple Museum.

Not only is this a site that records and preserves part of our American heritage, the New England Maple Museum is also one of the largest discount retailers of maple syrup in Vermont. More than 50,000 people pass through the gift shop each year, and the Christmas catalog goes out to more than 20,000. The regular catalog reaches at least 5,000.

The loyalty of the museum's customers attests to the excellent quality of its merchandise. There is a wide selection of gifts, candies, jams, and other maple products, including three grades of the world's finest maple syrup.

One pint of medium grade maple syrup is $10.95, and a 5.25-ounce box of maple candy is $6.95. Other sweets include maple drops for $5.25, maple nut fudge, 5.75, and peanut brittle 7.95. The museum also sells Side Hill Jam at $12.95 for four jars, and three cookbooks that feature treasured recipes of New England's finest cooks. Prices include shipping.

The New England Maple Museum also operates a retail shop in Pittsford that is open daily from March to December from 8:30 A.M. to 5:30 P.M.

Free catalog. Product guaranteed. Price quotes by letter or phone. Goods stocked and shipped by UPS or U. S. mail within one week. Will ship to Canada. Payment by American Express, MasterCard, Visa, check, or money order.

North Country Smokehouse

P. O. Box 1415
Claremont, New Hampshire 03743
(603) 543-0234

Praised by *The New York Times* for being "exemplary, light, fragrant and juicy . . . a very pleasant touch of sweetness," North Country meats are sold by such companies as L. L. Bean and Bloomingdale's.

The secret of North Country meats is in the special spicing and curing process that allows the spices to be fully absorbed, and a shorter time in a cob-and-maple smokehouse prevents a heavy creosote flavor that is so prevalent in other smoked meats.

The finest meats are selected for trimming by North Country's master butchers. The pork products are then cured in a secret blend of maple sugar and spices. The poultry is cured in a blend of brown sugar and spices. The sausages are mixed in accordance with old family recipes and left to steep in the spices for days until they are smoked and cooked. The hams, bacon, and turkeys are "pat down" in a cure of special seasonings and left for days in order to enhance the flavor of the meat.

North Country offers a full line of smoked meats: ham, bacon, Canadian bacon, pork loin, turkey breast, turkey, chicken breast, chicken, duck breast, duck, pheasant, Cornish game hen, trout, bluefish, Montreal

Praised by such publications as The New York Times *for being "exemplary, light, fragrant and juicy . . ."*

smoked meat, and kielbasa. They also carry smoked cheeses. If your favorite restaurant doesn't offer them, call North Country and order some today.

Free catalog. Wholesale available. Price quotes for wholesale only, by telephone. Product guaranteed. Goods stocked and shipped within three days by UPS, U.S. mail, or Federal Express. Payment by American Express, MasterCard, Visa, check or money order.

Boneless Ham	7-8 pounds	$55.00
Center Cut Ham Slices	3 pounds	24.00
Spareribs	3 pounds	24.00
Boneless Lamb	6 pounds	65.00
Boneless Turkey Breast	8 pounds	49.00
Brace of Pheasant		43.00

Ram Island Farm Herbs

Ram Island Farm
Cape Elizabeth, Maine 04107
(207) 767-5700

Ram Island Farm is a magical place. The farm is named for a tiny island just off the Maine coast, and is blessed with rich, fine soil and a relatively mild climate. It is a place where formal gardens and elegant old greenhouses compete with wild iris and lupin, and where the sea is a constant, living presence.

In this enchanting setting, Ric Marshall runs Ram Island Farm Herbs, offering his customers a wide selection of products that range from individually packaged herbs and spices and herb blends, through herbal vinegars and teas, to potpourri blends and bath oils and salts. All local herbs are organically grown and dried on the premises. Ric has his own unique recipes for the blends, but is ready to work with any customer's request for a special combination.

The quality of Ram Island Farm Herbs are recognized throughout New England, and are available in fine gourmet and gift shops in fifteen states, including the Museum Shops at the Smithsonian. In 1988 the Maine Christmas Potpourri was featured in the Christmas edition of The Horchow Collection.

Herbs and herb blends start at $3.50. Deep Rose Bath Salts are $6.00, and Bayberry Body Oil is $4.00.

Catalog service is available for $2.00, which includes two catalogs per year plus special mail offers. Wholesale available. Products stocked and shipped UPS within 24 hours of receipt. No credit cards accepted; telephone orders are shipped C.O.D. A $2.20 fee is charged for orders under $20.00.

Rathdowney, Ltd.

3 River Street, NE
P. O. Box 357
Bethel, Vermont 05032
(802) 234-9928 (inside Vermont)
(800) 543-8885 (outside Vermont)

In 1980 Louise and Brendan Downey-Butler bought a house on River Street in Bethel, Vermont, planning to live there and open a small business. Because of Louise's background in biology and her love of folklore and all growing things, they decided on a small herb shop. They had no idea of the success that was waiting for them.

When the store first opened, Louise made all the herb blends, food mixes, and recipe kits in small batches. She worked alone in the shop, occasionally taking her products to fairs and shows. The news spread quickly. Louise found her mailbox stuffed and her phone was always ringing.

Since the shop opened in 1982, Rathdowney, Ltd. has doubled its sales almost every year. The company now employs 22 people and has 4 retail locations, a mail order division, a large show circuit, and a wholesale trade with more than 3,000 accounts.

Rathdowney's products include a variety of herb blends and recipe kits, and such specialty items as popcorn seasoning, breakfast mixes, botanical posters, a flea-repelling carpet freshener, and Not Here Kitty!, a mix that keeps cats away from plants and furniture. They also publish their own cookbook, and a newsletter for their customers called *The New Thymes*.

Herbal recipe kits are $2.50 each or five for $10.00. Soup mixes make two quarts are are $3.95 each. Potpourri comes in one-half cup bags that are $2.00 each or three for $5.00.

Call or write for more information. Price quotes available by phone or letter. Products guaranteed. Most goods stocked; some made to order. Goods shipped UPS or U.S. mail within two weeks. Will ship to Canada. Payment by American Express, MasterCard, Visa, check, or money order.

Retail stores

| The Marketplace | 3 River St. | Timber Village | Kennedy Brothers |
| Bridgewater, VT | Bethel, VT | Quecher, VT | Vergennes, VT |

Rent Mother Nature

Department 992
P. O. Box 193
Cambridge, Massachusetts 02238
(617) 547-0657

If you are looking for an unusual gift, or just want to insure that you have the freshest food possible without moving to a farm, Rent Mother Nature will rent you a maple tree. Or lease you a lobster trap. Or sell you a time-share in a smokehouse.

These are not just gimmicks. They are real leases, signed, dated, and framed for you or as a gift for a friend. The pick of the crop is reserved for you, and Rent Mother Nature will deliver at least the guaranteed amount of maple syrup, lobsters, fruits, nuts, or honey stated in the lease.

This is how it works. A personalized lease document is sent to you which covers one of the Rent Mother Nature programs. As the months pass, you receive seasonal progress reports, updating information on the crops and weather. Finally, the harvest arrives, and the products are rushed to your door, guaranteeing you the freshest fruits, nuts, lobsters, syrup, or smoked meat possible.

Leases for maple trees start at $60.95, which guarantees at least 25 ounces of syrup. Hive leases are

$15.95, guaranteeing 20 ounces of honey. Lobsters traps are guaranteed to produce at least 6.5 pounds of lobsters for $134.50.

A lease on a pecan tree promises five pounds for $41.00. Apple tree leases guarantee one-half bushel for $37.00. A smokehouse time sharing program produces at least 3.5 to four pounds of ham, eight ounces of cheddar cheese, one pound of bacon and one pound of summer sausage for $87.00.

Catalog available for $1.00, refundable with purchase. Products guaranteed, shipped UPS or U.S. mail within one week of harvest. Most items can be shipped to Canada, excepts seafood and meats. Payment by American Express, MasterCard, Visa, check, or money order.

Roland & Son Custom Processed Meats

P. O. Box 278
South Barre, Vermont 05670
(802) 476-6066

For many years, this small family-owned business produced custom orders only and had a loyal following of customers. But as people moved away, and shared their Roland and Son treats with friends and relatives, the demand grew and a new mail order company was born.

With more than twenty years of experience and a strong background in the spice business, Roland and Son cob smokes and sells some of the most flavorful, most aromatic processed meats available.

They use corn cobs because cob smoke enhances the flavor of the meat without overpowering it. They use pure Vermont maple syrup as a sweetener and their own secret blend of spices. The result will tantalize your tongue and linger in your memory.

Roland and Son sells a line of ten products: boneless ham, bone-in ham, smoked boneless turkey breast, Vermont smoked beef, Canadian-style bacon, cob smoked pheasant, smoked boneless trout, cob smoked bacon, cob smoked sharp cheddar cheese (Cabot Sharp), and Vermont summer sausage.

Prices range from $6.55 for two 8-ounce bars of smoked cheddar cheese to $48.40 for an eight- to ten-pound whole boneless ham. A four to five pound

boneless turkey breast is $27.00, and a brace of pheasant is $43.00. Two pounds of sliced bacon is $11.55, and a four to five pound boneless ham is $25.45.

Prices include shipping for states east of the Mississippi, except for Florida.

Roland & Son operates a retail shop on Route 14 in South Barre that is open Monday through Friday from 8:00 A.M. to 5:00 P.M.

Free catalog. Wholesale available. No price quotes. Product guaranteed. Most goods are stocked; some custom orders. Shipped within two weeks by UPS. Payment by American Express, MasterCard, Visa, check, or money order.

Smith's Country Cheese

20 Otter River Road
Winchendon, Massachusetts 01475
(508) 939-5738

S mith's Country Cheese sells only one type: A high quality specialty Gouda cheese made right on their farm, using only rich, fresh milk from their own Holstein dairy herd. They use no colors or preservatives. The cheese is available plain, smoked, or with caraway seeds.

Gouda cheese originated in the Netherlands and has a mild flavor and small bubbly eyes. Although it is considered a dessert or appetizer cheese, it melts beautifully, and can be used on pizza, in quiches, omelets, hot dishes, and soups.

They sell the cheese by the pound or in gift packs that include such items as maple syrup, Raspberry Honey Poppyseed Mustard from Martha's Vineyard, preserves, flavored cheese spreads, smoked sausages, honey, and wafer breads. Cheese wedges start at $3.98 per pound, and gift packs are all under $50.00. Prices do not include shipping and handling.

The Smiths run a retail store at their farm on River Road in Winchendon that is open Monday through

Saturday from 10:00 A.M. to 5:00 P.M., and on Sunday 1:00 P.M. to 6:00 P.M. Their cheese is also available through specialty shops, farm stands, and grocery stores.

Free catalog. Wholesale available. Price quotes by letter or telephone. All cheeses and gift packs guaranteed and shipped within six days. Payment by Master-Card, Visa, or check.

State of Maine Cheese

75 Front Street
Dept. Tat
Rockland, Maine 04841
(207) 596-6601

Maine's only cheese company has a simple philosophy: "We love Maine pure and simple." Its contribution to Maine tradition is to take Maine milk from Maine cows pastured on Maine farms and make a cheddar cheese that's all natural with no preservatives.

They take their time and use diligent, time-honored methods, such as English hand cheddaring, to make a cheese worthy to carry the name of a state proud that its crafts are made by people who care.

Penobscot Cheddar
A delicate cheese made in the tradition of fine
English cheddars
Katahdin Cheddar
An all-natural, robust cheese that has been aged nine
months for a hearty flavor and sharp taste
Aroostook Jack
A natural version of the California cheese that has
a creamy texture and delicate taste
Sebago Gold
An old-fashioned washed curd cheese with a
Gouda-like flavor
Cumberland Smoked
A hardwood-smoked cheddar with a robust flavor
Allagash Caraway
A special blend of a natural Jack cheese and caraway
Kennebec Dill
A natural Jack cheese that has been spiced with dill
Saco Jalapeño
Mexico's most famous pepper has been added to
a natural Jack cheese to add a festive taste to any dish.

The cheeses come in a variety of sizes, and gift packs are offered to be used as company promotions. The five-pound gift pack is $19.50 and includes one 10-ounce bar each of Aroostook Jack, Kennebec Dill, Allagash Caraway, Saco Jalapeño, Cumberland Smoked Cheddar, Sebago Gold, Katahdin Cheddar and Penobscot Cheddar. They also offer three 10-ounce bars packaged in a distinctive wooden box for $14.00.

Free catalog. Wholesale available. Price quotes for large orders only, by letter or phone. Products guaranteed and shipped by UPS or U.S. mail. Will ship to Canada. Payment by MasterCard, Visa, check, or money order.

Sugarbush Farm

RFD 1, Box 568
Woodstock, Vermont 05091
(802) 457-1757

Personal service is characteristic of Sugarbush Farm. It's a small family business spanning three generations situated in a hundred-year-old farm house three miles up a country road. Customers are treated as real people. Betsy Ayres Luce types a personal note to go with each order. There are no computers and no answering machines.

Sugarbush Farm was started in 1945 by Jack and Marion Ayres. Today, it is run by their daughter Betsy and her husband Larry Luce. They encourage visitors to come and see them and "give you samples of our cheeses and maple syrup, and show you how we do things in the old Yankee tradition." The farm shop is situated three miles from Taftsville, which is three miles east of Woodstock on U.S. Route 4. Cross the covered bridge and follow the signs.

Photo by Jon Gilbert Fox

Each bar of Sugarbush Farm cheese is handwrapped in foil (a perfect moisture barrier), dipped twice in a special microcrystalline wax, and wrapped in cellophane—a unique wrapping process that keeps the cheese as fresh and moist as possible. Prices start at $7.10 for any foot-long bar (approximately one pound). They have six varieties:

Hickory and Maple Smoked
A delightful smooth cheese with plenty of smoked flavor
Sharp Cheddar
Approximately two years old and full of flavor and character
Sage Cheese
A mellow natural cheddar with flecks of herb sage
Mellow Cheddar
A creamy medium Vermont cheddar aged 6-10 months.
Green Mountain Jack
A mild cheese, an eastern variation of Monterey Jack.
Green Mountain Bleu
A rich creamy cheese, a big hit with all bleu cheese lovers.

In late February, Betsy and Larry hang two thousand sap buckets on the trees of Sugarbush farm. Working with the assistance of their workhorses, Jack and Clyde, who pull the sled filled with buckets. Betsy and Larry have to gather between 750 and 1,100 gallons of sap to make a 25-gallon batch of syrup.

One pint of syrup is $10.50, a quart is $16.25, a half gallon is $28.45. A half-pound jar of maple cream is $6.95; a nine-ounce package of maple sugar bon bons is $9.40; 1½ ounce maple leaf candies are $1.40 each; 1-pound jar pure honey $2.85. Prices do not include shipping and handling.

Free catalog. Wholesale available. Orders shipped UPS or U.S. mail same day of receipt. Will ship to Canada. Payment by American Express, MasterCard, Visa, Diners Club, check, or money order.

Trappist Abbey Gifts

St. Joseph's Abbey
Spencer, Massachusetts 01562
(508) 885-7011

For centuries, abbeys were known for the hospitality they extended to travelers. They offered shelter, and often a special meal beyond the simple fare of the monks who lived there.

Special treats St. Joseph's Abbey offered its guests were jams, jellies, and marmalades that were made on the premises. Today, the 80 monks of St. Joseph's extend that tradition of hospitality by making their more than 30 varieties of preserves available for anyone who wants to offer a special treat to family and friends.

Preserves come in three-ounce, eight-ounce, or 12-ounce jars that are shipped in pre-selected packs.

Personal selection packs are available only with 12-ounce jars. Prices for the personal selection packs start at $19.75 for four jars.

Prices for the pre-selected packs range from $7.90 for three three-ounce jars to $46.00 for 12 12-ounce jars. Prices include shipping charges and vary slightly according to shipping distance.

Free catalog. Wholesale available. No price quotes. Products guaranteed. Goods stocked and shipped UPS or U.S. mail within one week. Will ship to Canada. Payment by MasterCard, Visa, check, or money order.

Pure Fruit Preserves	Ginger Preserve	Seedless Red Raspberry Jam
Apricot Preserve	Grape Jelly	Seville Orange Marmalade
Apricot-Pineapple Preserve	Lemon Marmalade	Strawberry Jelly
Blackberry Seedless Jam	Peach Preserve	Strawberry Preserve
Blueberry Preserve	Peach with Sherry	Sweet Orange Marmalade
Boysenberry Seedless Jam	Quince Jelly	
Cherry Preserve	Red Currant Jelly	*Wine Jellies*
Cranberry Conserve	Red Raspberry Jam	Burgundy
Damson Plum Jam	Rhubarb-Orange Conserve	Port
Elderberry Jelly	Rhubarb-Strawberry Preserve	Rose
Fig Preserve	Seedless Black Raspberry Jam	Sherry

Westfield Farm

28 Worcester Road
Hubbardston, Massachusetts 01452
(508) 928-5110

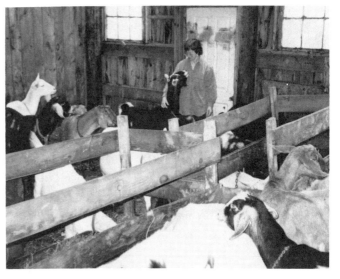

I f you ever get a craving for fresh Capri goat cheese in the middle of the night, there's a place half a mile south of Hubbardston Center, Massachusetts, that can help. The shop at Westfield Farm's cheesemaking plant is open 7 days a week, 24 hours a day. It's self-service.

Bob and Letty Kilmoyer worked for more than ten years to perfect the process for making some of the finest goat cheeses in America. They raise their own Nubian and Saanen goats, milk them twice a day, and make a cheese that can be shipped to the customer fresh within days.

The award-winning cheeses are shipped in insulated containers packed with ice. Their specialties are the Capri and Herb Garlic Capri Cheeses, but their selection also includes a Pepper Capri, Hubbardston Blue, Camembert, and Blue Log. Prices start at $1.75 for a 4 oz. log.

Free catalog. Wholesale available. Price quotes by letter or phone. Goods are stocked, with some made to order. Shipped UPS (2nd day air is used for long distance shipping) within three days. Payment by check or money order.

The Whip and Spoon

161 Commercial Street
Portland Maine, 04101
(207) 774-4020

The Whip and Spoon was started to celebrate the best homemade foods that Maine has to offer. They have strived to gather the best and most interesting products and have personally tasted and tested each one.

Some products are already packaged, but if you need an extra special gift for one friend, or gifts for fifty business associates, they can fill your order. They will fill the baskets for you, or you can request a selection of any of their wide collection of Maine delicacies.

The Whip and Spoon has retail stores at 161 Commerical Street in Portland and at 198 Maine Mall Road in South Portland. Call for hours.

Free brochure. Products guaranteed. Shipped UPS within 48 hours of receipt. Payment by American Express, MasterCard, Visa, check, or money order.

Maine Berries
Picked by Nancy Ward and made into jam by Nancy in her own kitchen. Three 8-ounce jars for $17.95.

Blue Ribbon Relish
Downeast Delicacies' 12-ounce New England Cranberry-Apple Relish has a smooth and chunky texture with a tart and sweet flavor.

Good Morning from Maine
A package of wildflower honey, blueberry and black raspberry jams, and maple syrup in a 9" woven basket. $18.95.

Downeast Coffee Break
A 12-ounce jar of Red Tomato Marmalade and 1½ pounds of organically grown and stone ground whole wheat and toasted buckwheat muffin mix. $10.95.

Tastes of Maine
A wooden lobster trap filled with Sugar Tree Farm Amber Maple Syrup, Mother's Mountain Original and new Portland Beer Mustard, Gary Gauvin's Blueberry Jam, and a Haven's Candy Kitchen Chocolate Lobster. $25.95.

Blueberry Placemats
Hand stenciled, 100% handwoven catton mats. Two for $10.95.

100% Pure Maple Syrup
Collected at the Sugar Tree Farm in Jackman, Maine. One quart is $19.95. A half gallon is $36.95.

Wood's Cider Mill

RD 2, Box 477
Springfield, Vermont 05156
(802) 263-5547

Willis and Tina Wood have a simple business. On a farm that has been in the family since 1798, they raise a few cows, sheep, and chickens, and keep a small garden. And they ship five farm-made items to satisfied customers all over the country.

Each fall, the Woods crush and press up to ten thousand bushels of apples to make their cider jelly and boiled cider. Neither product has any added sweeteners or preservatives. Boiled cider is concentrated about seven to one, and cider jelly about nine to one. Boiled cider is used with hot water for a delightful hot drink, in cooking (it's a great ham glaze), or as a topping for pancakes, yogurt, or ice cream. Cider jelly makes a great peanut butter and jelly sandwich, and is good on muffins and toast or with a meat dish.

The Woods tap more than two thousand trees for their maple syrup, which they sell in its pure form or blended with their boiled cider for a delicious cider syrup.

They also sell the yarn from their small flock of sheep. The yarn is not dyed, just spun into soft, water-repellent two-ply skeins. Therefore, only two colors are available, off-white and black. The yarn is sold by the ounce, looped in four-ounce skeins, with approximately 250 yards per pound.

One pint of maple syrup is $7.50. One pint of cider syrup is $6.50, and one pint of boiled cider is $5.00. A pack of four eight-ounce jars of cider jelly is $8.50.

Products can be bought at the farm.

Free catalog. Minimum order of four 8-ounce jars. Wholesale available. Goods shipped by UPS, unless otherwise requested, within one week. Goods are stocked and guaranteed. Will ship to Canada. Payment by check.

As
YOU
LIKE IT

HOMES AND
HOME FURNISHINGS

Jas. Becker, Cabinetmaker

"A" Street
P. O. Box 802
Wilder, Vermont 05088
(802) 295-7004

In the fall of 1980, Jim Becker began working with Thos. Moser Cabinetmakers in New Gloucester, Maine. After building chairs, benches, and custom pieces for more than five years, he moved to Lebanon, New Hampshire, and opened his own shop. Since opening, Jim has produced furniture in many styles, and almost 50 percent of his work has been commissions for original designs.

Whether the customer is an architect with a detailed blueprint or someone with a vague idea, Jim will work closely with the customer to bring the piece of furniture into existence. He can reproduce an original antique, make an adaption of a contemporary piece, or he can design a unique piece, from banquet tables to deacon's benches.

Prices range for existing pieces range from $700.00 for his contemporary Windsor side chair to $4,200.00 for a cherry open back hutch. Other items include a contemporary cabriole-leg dining table for $3,000.00, a deacon's bench for $1,750.00, a coffee table with drawer for $1,250.00, and Hope's huntboard for $3,650.00.

Jas. Becker Cabinetmaker maintains a display in the Galleria Mall in Hanover, New Hampshire. Jim's shop is now in Wilder, Vermont, and is open Tuesday through Friday from 8:00 A.M. to 5:30 P.M. or by appointment. Please call ahead if possible. Jim works alone, and the shop is closed any time Jim is not there.

Free catalog. Products guaranteed. Price quotes by letter or phone. Some goods are stocked; most are made to order. Ships by UPS or common carrier. Will ship to Canada. Shipping time varies. Payment by check or money order.

Bennington Potters

P. O. Box 99
127 College Street
Burlington, Vermont 05402
(802) 863-2221

Since 1948 Bennington Potters has been designing and producing a line of stoneware that feels comfortable and looks smart in a variety of settings from contemporary to traditional to country. They have created a line that carries their built-in signature: a strength of design with heirloom durability.

The Vermont pottery where all cookware is designed and manufactured also contains a restaurant where the chef tests and has the last word on the usefulness of each piece. Thus, their cookware is beautiful and tough with restaurant durability and usefulness.

They also have a beautiful terracotta collection of planters, hanging baskets, plant stands, and birdfeeders.

The Bennington Potters retail shop at 127 College Street in Burlington handles all their mail orders. Call (802) 863-2221 for mail order and hours that the shop is open. A second retail shop is at their factory, located at 324 County Street in Bennington. Call (802) 447-7531 for hours.

Catalog available for $1.00, refundable with purchase. Wholesale available. Price quotes by letter or phone. Products guaranteed with proper use. Most goods are stocked. Ships UPS (U.S. mail on request) within eight weeks, although two to six weeks is the average shipping time. Payment by MasterCard, Visa, check, or money order. Checks must have major credit card guarantee.

Agate Dinnerware	
12-ounce Mug	$ 7.50
8.5-inch Luncheon Plate	12.00
10.5-inch Buffet Plate	15.00
Medium Bowl with Rim	48.00
Cook's Ware	
10-inch Dinner Plate	13.00
Lasagna Dish	25.00
Bread Pan	18.00
Medium Mixing Bowl	15.00
Terracotta	
Medium Hanging Planter	11.00
Medium Square Planter with Stand	18.00
Large Round Zigguarat	30.00
Walking Ducks	29.00

Deborah Bump, Sculptor

RFD 3, Box 254
Putney, Vermont 05436
(802) 387-4320

The unique, often whimsical, sculpture/boxes of Deborah Bump have been evolving for more than 20 years. Birds, animals, and fish have always been her chosen subjects, and she tries to show animal life in a way that will grab attention and prod us to see more of life around us. The color and texture of wood make it a fine medium for this task.

Sometimes humorous, sometimes an abstraction of characteristic elements, sometimes a movement frozen in time, the sculptures are based on study, observation, and drawing in natural settings, in zoos and museums, and in books.

Her blue whales are an elegant pair—dad and baby—that capture the sleek majesty of the whale.

The moose is an apt portrait of the ponderous creature with its knobby legs and broad feet.

The beaver family is just out of the water with a streamline profile and comic overbite.

The kangaroos are a flaky pair with fur trim and one drawer and one joey each.

The rhino and hippo are finely detailed sculptures of two of the most regal animals in her collection.

Each sculpture is treated as a separate piece, thus assuring the mark of individual quality which has always distinguished Deborah's work. The sculptures are made of various woods, including cherry, walnut, mahogany, and maple. Each is naturally finished with non-toxic materials, and each comes with a descriptive tag. Most of the sculptures have a box or drawer incorporated into the animal, ideal for jewelry or small desk items.

Please write or call for more information. Most items stocked; commissions considered. Orders acknowledged promptly. Sculptures will be delivered by UPS within four weeks.

Dad Beaver	$60.00
Mom Beaver	45.00
Kit Beaver	40.00
Big Blue Whale	90.00
Baby Blue Whale	55.00
Goose, various poses	75.00
Hippo with drawer	75.00
Kangaroo	200.00
Owl, 2 drawers	70.00
Owl, 3 drawers	175.00
Siegfried (Sea Dragon)	175.00

Cape Cod Braided Rug

259 Great West Road
Box 495
South Dennis, Massachusetts 02660
(508) 398-0089

For four generations the Paulus family has been making braided rugs. They braid the finest materials available into one-inch strips, then braid them again before sewing. Most modern rug manufacturers skip that first and most important step.

Although they have a lot of rugs in stock—their store has the largest selection in Massachusetts—the Paulus family specialty is custom-made rugs, handcrafted to customers' specifications. Send them your wall paper scrap or paint chip or just a photo. Talk to them about what you have in mind, and they will design a rug to accent or highlight any room.

Every Cape Cod Braided Rug carries the Paulus tradition of handcrafted excellence and quality. They will be happy to answer any question. Feel free to call them any time.

They also offer decorative accessories such as chair pads, deacon's bench pads, stair treads, rocker sets, place mats, candles, and baskets.

Standard size rugs are either oval or round. Rugs are made up to 13 feet in any dimension. Prices range from $37.50 for a 2 x 3 oval rug to $729.00 for a 9 x 12 oval. Odd size rugs will be made at $6.75 a square foot (length x width x $6.75).

Retail store on site.

Catalog available for $1.00. Products guaranteed. Price quotes by letter or phone. Goods shipped by UPS within eight weeks. Will ship to Canada. Payment by MasterCard, Visa, or check.

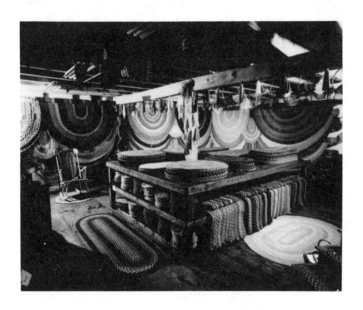

Colors Available			
White	Brown	Dark Blue	Yellow
Light Green	Red	Beige	Pink
Brick	Navy	Cranberry	Wine
Camel	Rose	Light Blue	Gray
Dark Green	Rust	Colonial Blue	Cocoa
Avocado Black			

Cape Cod Cupola

78 State Road
North Dartmouth, Massachusetts 02747-2994
(508) 994-2119

Since Deacon Shem Drowne placed a copper grasshopper on top of Fanueil Hall in 1749, Boston has been the home of more weathervanes than any other American city. Even though many of the older vanes have been taken down, Boston still has a number of old vanes that have faced down the wind since the eighteenth century.

Although no one knows for certain when the first weathervane was built in America, some historians believe they were made in this country as early as 1690. The making of handcrafted weathervanes is part of our American heritage.

Cape Cod Cupola has been a part of that tradition since 1939. Their copper and aluminum weathervanes feature traditional and contemporary designs in both silhouette and full-body forms. They use individual animals, people, and ships as well as small vignettes of life in days past.

They also feature a full line of cupolas on which to mount your weathervane. All cupolas are made of pine and handpainted with two coats of exterior white paint. The roof is covered with aluminum or copper.

In addition, Cape Cod Cupola offers a wide selection of home accessories such as wall decor, mailbox signs, sundials, yard signs, weather forecasting instruments, welcome plaques, even bookmarks. Prices for weathervanes range from $32.50 for an all-aluminum vane with a black finish to $812.00 for a full-bodied copper horse. Prices for the cupolas range from $152.00 for an unfinished aluminum model to $1,892.00 for a custom made Mount Vernon model with a copper roof.

The craftspeople at Cape Cod Cupola operate a retail shop on site. They are open Monday through Friday from 8:00 A.M. to 4:30 P.M., and on weekends by appointment.

Catalog available for $2.00, refundable with purchase of more than $10.00. Wholesale available. Price quotes by letter only. Products are guaranteed. Custom orders not returnable. Most goods stocked; some made to order. Shipped UPS or common carrier. Shipping time depends on the time of year. Will ship to Canada. Payment by MasterCard, Visa, check, or money order.

Christian Ridge Pottery and Tile Works

RR #1, Box 252
South Paris, Maine 04281
(207) 743-8419

The Christian Ridge potters are constantly trying to come up with something new. In addition to their extensive line of handcrafted tableware, trivets, and lamps in distinctive and original designs, they have used their imagination to create the Bakato™, an ingenious gourmet dish that bakes by conducting heat to the heart of a potato through its special cooking spikes. Great for a one-dish meal, this unusual dish can be used in the microwave or in a conventional oven.

They also developed the original Apple Baker®, and have designed distinctive mugs, spoon rests, mixing bowls, and other kitchen accessories, as well as lamps, planters, cabinet knobs, and door pulls.

In addition to the cookware, Christian Ridge has a line of tiles. Made from red earthenware clay, the tiles are tough enough to withstand decades of use on floors, countertops, showers, hearths, and walls. Christian Ridge tiles are created in designs unavailable anywhere else.

Their standard tiles come in four shapes, in nine sizes, and in more than 20 colors. They will also produce custom tiles to fit any requirements, creating a design for your location.

Free catalog. Some goods in stock; some made to order. Shipped UPS or U.S. mail. Shipping time varies. Payment by MasterCard, Visa, check, or money order.

Pottery		
Apple Baker®	Boxed Pair	$15.00
Bakato™	Boxed Pair	15.00
Dinnerware Set	5-piece setting	56.00
Pitcher	1-pint size	16.00
Pie or Quiche Dish	9-inch size	24.00
Door Pull		10.00
Cabinet Knob		6.00
Table Lamp	Small base	45.00

Tile Colors		
Snow White	Tile Green	Speckled Blue
Yellow Chiffon	Forest Green	Blush Tan
Mustard	Sea Foam	Grey Flannel
Butternut	Midnight Blue	Mocha
Snow Pink	Steel Blue	Chocolate Bar
Pink	Grotto Blue	Fudge
Raspberry Fizz	Periwinkle	Naugahyde
Antique Rose	African Violet	Coffee Bean

The Clown Factory

P. O. Box 696
Assonet, Massachusetts 02702
(508) 678-4150

Everybody loves a clown," and Mary Berlo's Clown Factory makes clowns to suit everybody's sense of humor.

There's "Emmet," the sad-faced circus clown, dressed in plaid clothes and carrying a hobo stick and pouch.

"Pierete" and "Pierrot," the French harlequins with delicate faces and clothes of fine cotton, make a great engagement or shower gift.

As a gift for a newborn, "Baby Girl Pink" or "Baby Boy Blue" will make a keepsake to be cherished for years to come.

The Clown Factory also makes "occupation" clowns such as "The Fisherman," "Combat Joey," "The Cowboy," and "The Fireman," and the perky "Rainbow" and "Nicky," circus clowns with ever-changing faces.

Some of the Clown Factory's best sellers, however, are their holiday dolls. "John and Priscilla," their Pilgrim dolls; "The Witch" with her broom and pointed felt hat; and "Mrs. Claus" and "Santa Claus," keepsakes that make a delightful addition to any holiday decor.

Every one of the Clown Factory's clowns are handcrafted of the finest materials and made with much love and care. The clowns have a wooden core for stability and a soft cotton cover that allows Mary to design each one with a different character and personality. The clowns are appproximately two feet tall and sit alone with arms and legs that can be moved to different poses—not toys, but charming collectors' items. They make great gifts or provide a finishing touch to any decor.

Most of the clowns are available for $19.95. "Emmet" is $24.95, and "Santa Claus," "Mrs. Claus," and the "Country Lady" are $29.95.

Catalog available for $2.00, refundable with purchase. Products guaranteed. Goods are stocked and shipped by UPS or U. S. mail within eight weeks. Will ship to Canada. Payment by check or money order.

Cohasset Colonials

38 Parker Avenue
Cohasset, Massachusetts 02025
(617) 383-0110

In 1938, a love of woodworking and rowing led Francis Hagerty to establish a business on Cohasset Harbor building rowing shells. He built a successful business by following three principles: make the boats correctly, educate customers about them, and provide service when they need help.

In 1949, intrigued by the joinery of antique furniture, Francis introduced America's first museum reproduction furniture kits. They were such a success that the focus of his business changed, but his adherence to his three basic principles did not.

Those principles, hard work, and attention to detail have built a reputation for Cohasset Colonials as design purists. They have been asked to renovate some of America's historic inns and taverns, and have reproduction rights to fine furniture pieces from Colonial Williamsburg, The Metropolitan Museum of Art, The Concord Antiquarian Museum, Fruitlands Museum, Congress Hall, Shelburne Museum, and Wadsworth Atheneum.

To verify its authenticity, each piece is branded with the Cohasset mark and includes the name of the institution holding the original.

Kits range from simple chests, trays, and sconces, to highboys, dining room suites, and four-poster beds. They also offer accessories such as artwork, tableware, and lamps to accent your newly-created reproductions.

In 1977, following Francis Hagerty's unexpected death, his youngest son, John, took over the company, carrying on the family tradition of a business founded on quality, education, and service.

Catalog available for $3.00. Price quotes available by phone or letter. Kits shipped by UPS within 7 days. Will ship to Canada. Payment by American Express, MasterCard, Visa, or checks.

	Kit	Assembled
Bowback Windsor Armchair	$258.00	$439.00
Birdcage Windsor Sidechair	169.00	298.00
Birdcage Windsor Armchair	194.00	359.00
Four-Post Canopy Bed-Queen	559.00	898.00
Shaker Table	79.00	159.00
Connecticut Valley Tea Table	159.00	259.00

FOUR DRAWER CHIPPENDALE CHEST 650

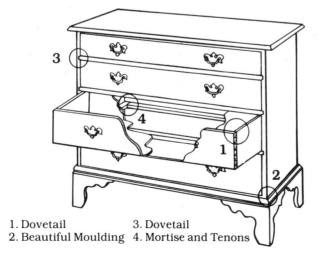 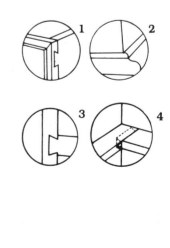

1. Dovetail   3. Dovetail
2. Beautiful Moulding   4. Mortise and Tenons

Colonial Country Originals

P. O. Box 2010
193 Rockland Street
Hanover, Massachusetts 02339
(617) 826-7708

Colonial Country Originals is a manufacturer of quality colonial reproduction curtains sold under the Constance Carol brand name. Each curtain is custom made. All fabrics are hand selected and each pair of curtains is individually stitched with meticulous attention to detail. These are the finest curtains available. They also carry all the hardware needed to hang the curtains to their best advantage.

Colonial Country Originals features four basic styles of Early American curtains: Tab, Sash, Shaker, and Continental. These four styles are offered in a wide variety of fabrics, designs, and trims, such as Patrician Strip, Lorraine Festoon, Trimmed Shaker, and Stenciled Cafe.

They also carry a selection of braided rugs or will custom make one to match your curtains or wallpaper.

Colonial Country Originals is a small family-run business that is striving for customer satisfaction, not volume, so each curtain is made only after the order is received. They can't ship it to you within 24 hours, but they'll notify you if it's going to take longer than four weeks, and if you don't like the finished product, you can return it for immediate credit, refund, or exchange.

Their business philosophy is simple and old fashioned: "Never compromise on quality and treat the customer right."

Free catalog. Products guaranteed. Goods are made to order, usually shipped within four weeks by UPS or parcel post. Will ship to Canada. Payment by Master-Card, Visa, check, or money order.

Curtain	Length	Width	Price
Tom Thumb Ruffles	90	45 or 54	$41.00
Newfield Tabs	80	72	75.00
Darby	80	54	83.00
Hand Stenciled	80	36 or 40	57.00
Country Swags	40	38 or 43	32.00
Shaker	80	36 or 40	67.00

Trimmed Shaker Curtain

Tab Curtain

Sash Curtain

Country Wenham

Cooper Hill Quiltworks

P. O. Box 345
Johnson, Vermont 05656
(802) 635-7880

S ince 1974, Cooper Hill Quiltworks has been designing and producing the most versatile, longest-wearing, and most decorative quilts in New England. Their wide range of colors and designs, from the fiercely traditional Log Cabin and Victorian Medallion to the strikingly modern Pineapple adaptation, means there is a Cooper Hill quilt appropriate for virtually any bed or decor.

Made exclusively in northern Vermont, each quilt is handpieced, double-stitched for strength, and hand-tied. Crafted from the finest quality cottons and cotton blend fabrics, the quilts are filled with a bonded polyester batting, and completely machine washable.

The deep, rich colors, vibrant contrasts, and precise craftsmanship that make these quilts distinctive also appear in their bedding accessories. You can furnish your bed with matching or coordinating pillow shams and dust ruffles.

They have a large number of quilts and bed dressings in stock, but eagerly welcome custom and contract work. Cooper Hill quilts decorate some of the finest inns in New England.

Let Cooper Hill craft a quilt that will take a place of pride in your home.

Catalog for $2.00, refundable with purchase. Price quotes only for custom work. Quilts are shipped within eight weeks. Will ship to Canada and overseas. Prices of quilts do not include shipping. Payment by MasterCard, Visa, or check.

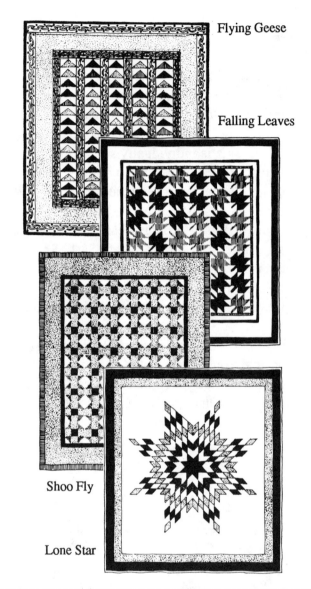

Flying Geese

Falling Leaves

Shoo Fly

Lone Star

Pattern	Twin	Double/Queen	King
God's Eye	$220.00	$270.00	$330.00
Shadows	265.00	315.00	375.00
Flying Geese	270.00	340.00	415.00
Falling Leaves	295.00	370.00	455.00
Shoo Fly	330.00	385.00	485.00
Log Cabin	390.00	475.00	560.00

Country Curtains

At the Red Lion Inn
Stockbridge, Massachusetts 01262
(413) 243-1474

When Jane and Jack Fitzpatrick started Country Curtains more than 30 years ago, they began with one style of curtain. When they moved to Stockbridge two years later, all the curtains fit into the back of a station wagon, and their new house had only one room set aside for the business.

The word began to spread, however, of the beauty of the curtains and the dedication that Jane and Jack had to their customers' happiness. Today, they have a thriving mail order business and ten retail shops in New England and New Jersey.

Swag Over Tier

Free catalog. Write or call 24 hours a day. They are closed on Christmas Day. Products guaranteed. Goods are stocked and shipped UPS or parcel post. Federal Express service available. Will ship to Canada. Payment by MasterCard, Visa, check, or money order.

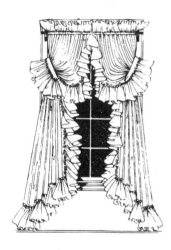
Tied Back with Deep Ruffle Tiebacks

The Country Curtains catalog today contains more than 50 pages of curtains. Styles include colonial and federal, Irish lace and cottage ruffles, balloon tiers, and lace sheers. Country Curtains has a selection waiting for you. And if you aren't sure of a fabric or color, they will send you free fabric swatches. They also carry 100 percent softspun cotton afghans and "Theo," the huggable cuddly bear.

Country Curtains still considers their dedication to their customers to be one of their strongest selling points. They give you individual attention and you can return anything that isn't quite right for a refund or exchange. Curtain prices start at $16.50 per pair.

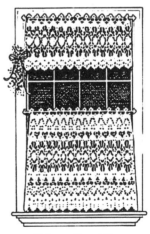
Valance Over Tier

Balloon Curtain 4001	$59.00 per panel
Tapered Valance 2001	9.00 each
Victorian Ruffles 9037	87.00 per pair
Wide Eyelet Ruffles EH1	55.00 per pair
Heirloom Lace 6038	20.50 per pair
Irish Lace Ruffles 4211	12.00 each

The Different Drummer

P. O. Box 374
East Windsor, Connecticut 06088
(203) 627-0494 (9:30 A.M. to 4:30 P.M.)
(203) 627-0344 (after 4:30 P.M.)

The Different Drummer is a family-owned business that carries two separate product lines.

The first is an extensive line of Pennsylvania Dutch Hex Signs and related material such as trivets, stencils, informational booklets, and novelty items. From the Pineapple Hospitality hex to the intricate Love Star, the exquisite, handpainted hex signs wish success and love. The hand-crafted trivets and lawn signs offer sentimental or humorous messages such as "To love and be loved is the greatest joy on earth," and "The more I see of some people the better I like my dog."

The second product line from the Different Drummer features a wide selection of handcarved and handpainted wooden wall hangings and name signs made to the specifications of the customer.

Because each sign is individually made, no two are exactly alike. All signs are made of northern pine boards that are three-quarters of an inch thick. Carved signs are finished with a medium dark stain to highlight the grain of the woods, and covered with a semi-gloss lacquer that resists water. Handpainted signs are completed with a semi-gloss polyurethane varnish. All signs can be displayed outdoors, although they should be protected from direct rain or snow.

Prices for handcarved signs range from $21.00 to $46.00. Handpainted signs range from $18.00 to $30.00. Hex signs are available in three different sizes: the 8-inch size is $4.00, the sixteen-inch size is $7.00, and the twenty-four-inch size is $14.00

Catalog for product lines available for $1.00 each (specify if you want the hex sign or wall signs catalog), refundable with purchase. Wholesale available. Products guaranteed. Price quotes for name signs only, by letter. All goods stocked, except for name signs. Ships UPS (parcel post by request) within four weeks. Will ship to Canada. Payment by MasterCard, Visa, check, or money order.

Donnell's Clapboard Mill

RR 1, Box 1560
Sedgwick, Maine 04676
(207) 359-2036

Pine clapboards are one reason that some seventeenth and eighteenth century homes are still standing. Clapboards hold stains and paint better than any other surface and give a home a dignified, historical appearance unmatched by any other siding.

For a long time, this durable siding was almost unavailable, but using restored 19th-century machinery, Donnell's Clapboard Mill has revived the neglected art of milling radially-sawn clapboards.

Commonly called "quarter-sawn," clapboards were originally hand split from short logs. The industrial revolution brought the making of clapboards into the mill, although short logs were still the standard. Donnell's Clapboard Mill was the first and only mill to use 8' logs.

The logs are first turned on Donnell's old clapboard log lathe to remove all bark and irregularities. It is then moved to the clapboard saw, which cuts into the log. After each cut the log is rotated for the next cut. The clapboards are removed from the log's core and stacked in piles for air drying, which retains and preserves the wood's natural oils and preservatives. After drying, the clapboards are planed for smoothness and trimmed for a close fit and easy installation.

Because of this traditional milling process, clapboards do not warp or twist. They lie flat, tight, even, and smooth for decades.

Clapboards are available in two grades. The #1 premium clear clapboards have no knots, pitch pockets, or other blemishes, and are ideal for restoration or custom designed modern home. The #2 New England Cape clapboards may have some small solid or "pin" knots, or an occasional worm hole or pitch pockets. These are suitable for repair work or for smaller buildings that are going to be painted.

In addition to standard clapboard sizes, special sizes can be cut to meet the needs for an unusual repair job or an unique home design.

Donnell's operates a retail shop at the mill. Call for hours.

Catalog available for $1.00. Clapboards are shipped in bundles of 48 linear feet by common carrier. Payment by check or money order.

Grade	Size	Price/Linear Foot
#1 Premium Clear Pine	5 1/2"	$1.19
#2 New England Cape Pine	5 1/2"	1.04
#1 Premium Clear Pine	4 1/2"	.97
#2 New England Cape Pine	4 1/2"	.87
#1 Premium Clear Pine	6"	1.48

Ebenezer Flagg Company

65 Touro Street
Newport, Rhode Island 02840
(401) 846-1891

The Ebenezer Flagg Company is a full service flag and banner store. They stock an extensive line of state, national, and historic flags, specialty flags for holidays, miniature flags, flag sets, religious flags, windsocks and yacht flags, and wall hangings.

They also make custom flags following customers' designs. You can put your company logo or personal coat-of-arms on a flag or banner.

All flags and banners are made from Annin fabrics. For more than five generations, Annin flags and fabrics have been recognized as the standard of quality throughout the world. Annin is the official supplier of flags to all branches of the United States federal government and all branches of the armed services. Their reputation of excellence is maintained by a dedication to careful attention to each manufacturing detail by men and women highly skilled in their craft and proud of their work.

By offering their customers flags of Annin fabrics, Ebenezer Flagg insures that every customer receives a durable as well as a beautiful treasure.

Flags can be made for indoor or outdoor use. Prices for custom flags start at $216.00. The prices on historic United States flags range from $19.30 to $30.90. State flags for indoor use range from $35.40 to $78.50. State flags for outdoor use range from $9.90 to $97.90.

The Ebenezer Flagg Company operates a retail shop at 65 Touro Street in Newport that is open Monday through Friday from 8:30 A.M. to 5:00 P.M.; Saturday from 10:00 A.M. to 5:00 P.M.; Sunday from 12:00 P.M. to 5:00 P.M.

Catalog available for $2.50. Products guaranteed. Price quotes by letter or phone. Some goods stocked; some made to order. Ships UPS or U.S. mail within six weeks. Will ship to Canada. Payment by MasterCard, Visa, check, or money order.

Ian Eddy, Blacksmith

RFD 1, Box 975
Putney, Vermont 05346
(802) 387-5991

I an Eddy's wife, Jenny, came to America from England when she was 18. On a 1970 visit to her grandfather, Col. Garton, in Somerset, England, Ian was inspired by the work produced by Col. Garton's smithy.

After completing his bachelor's degree, Ian opened a blacksmith shop in 1975. His business has grown steadily, his work can be found in shops and galleries throughout the United States, and he has been commissioned to do architectural work for private homes. He produces a wide selection of home accessories, from small plant hooks and utensil racks, bathroom hooks and towel bars, paper towel holders and skewer sets, to fireplace tools and chandeliers. Prices start at less than $10.00. Ian encourages custom work.

Ian, Jenny, and Matthew Eddy live and work in a music-filled home on a terraced hillside in Putney surrounded by flowers and vegetables, horses, dogs, and cats. Dedicated to living a joyful, self-sufficient life, they continually strive for refinement and discovery of new designs.

Free catalog. Wholesale available. Most goods stocked; some made to order. Goods shipped UPS (C.O.D. on request).

Swinging Ring Plant Hanger	$48.00
Swivel Plant Hanger	17.00
Arch Bracket Plant Hanger	53.00
S Hook	4.50
Rolling Pin Hook	6.50
Serpent Paper Towel Holder	35.00
Heart Paper Towel Holder	24.00
18-inch Medium Heart Towel Bar	24.50
Ring Towel Bar	17.50
Poker, ⅜ Square	19.00
Shovel, ⅜ Round Simple	21.00
3-Hook Fireplace Tool Stand	95.00
Heart Hanging Utensil Rack	55.00
Skewer	7.00
Small Heart Sconce	31.00
4-Arm Chandelier	220.00
Door Knocker	37.00
Heart Trivet	37.00

Ellie May Swing Company

P. O. Box 228
Sharon, Massachusetts 02067
(800) 458-1859 (outside Massachusetts)
(617) 784-8535 (inside Massachusetts)

There's something about a porch swing that recalls memories of soft summer evenings, of listening to crickets and waiting for the dew to fall and the fireflies to come out. Even when porches gave way to suburban stoops, porch swings were hung in A-frames.

The Ellie May Swing Company preserves this gentle tradition, adding a touch of New England quality. All their porch swings and outdoor furniture are handcrafted of the finest woods, following New England standards of design and durability.

Generous and comfortable contoured seats and backs are featured in Classic or Contemporary styles. Using teak or Honduras mahogany for their outdoor pieces and constructing their under-cover swings in oiled white oak, they create furniture of solid heirloom quality that will withstand years of weather and wear.

They offer traditional flat-arm swings or contemporary curved-arm swings in three-, four-, or five-foot sizes with prices that range from $159.00 for a three-foot flat-arm in white oak to $339.00 for a five-foot curved-arm in mahogany.

They also offer complementary benches, chairs, and planters. Each piece is handcrafted, one at a time, so they can make custom sized furniture

Catalog available for $1.00, refundable with purchase. Products guaranteed. Most items are stocked, some made to order. Ships within two weeks by UPS or air or motor freight. Payment by MasterCard, Visa, check, or money order.

J. Donald Felix, Coppersmith

P. O. Box 995
Hampton, New Hampshire 03842
(603) 474-2225

Once a traditional and useful part of any home, weathervanes were handmade and as individual as the homes and farms they were on. As they became more popular, however, the greater demand led to cast-iron molds and mass production.

J. Donald Felix has revived the art of the weathervane. Don hand raises each piece using a long hammering process without the use of any molds, giving each weathervane the individual character of a fine work of art.

The weathervanes are made from the finest copper and brass and tell true wind direction. They are strong enough to stand up to the elements for generations, but because of the high quality, more and more are being found inside the home as often as they are on top.

Custom work is Don's specialty. He can make any style using only a picture. He also makes distinctive wall hangings, candle sconces, and other sculptures. Prices for most weathervanes and sculptures start around $300.

Catalog available for $1.00, refundable with purchase. Most items are made to order and shipped by UPS or U.S. mail within ten weeks. Will ship to Canada. Product guaranteed. Payment by check or money order.

The Good Time Stove Company

Rte 112, Box 306
Goshen, Massachusetts 01032
(413) 268-3677

For centuries, the heart of the American home was the wood or coal burning stove that heated the house and cooked the food. Today, many people think of these wonderful iron masterpieces as nostalgic antiques, or—at best—something to use when the electricity goes off.

Richard "Stove Black" Richardson views these stoves as functional works of art, and since 1973 he has been restoring and selling stoves and ranges that date back to 1790. "Built before an era of planned obsolescence, these stoves have been proven to withstand the test of time. These stoves add warmth and character and enhance any home." Working at a shop deep in the Massachusetts Berkshires, where heating with wood has been a way of life for generations, Stove Black offers his customers the best of our past for a lasting future.

Good Time Stoves are authentic antique wood and coal-burning stoves and wood or wood/gas combination kitchen ranges. The stoves are fully restored and ready to fire and are as efficient to use as they are lovely to look at. And for those who want the appearance of an old stove but the convenience of electricity, Stove Black will convert an antique stove into an electric version.

The prices of the stoves vary according to size and type of stove and the amount and style of restoration. Most of the stoves start at approximately $1,000.00.

Retail shop at site, open by appointment only. Video tape on buying a stove available for $20.00, refundable when tape is returned.

Free catalog. Wholesale available. Price quotes by letter. Products stocked and guaranteed. Shipped U.S. mail and motor freight. Will ship to Canada. Payment by MasterCard, Visa, or money order.

Hampshire Pewter

P. O. Box 1570
Wolfeboro, New Hampshire 03864
(603) 569-4944

In 1983 Hampshire Pewter was asked to create Christmas ornaments for the New Hampshire tree on the Ellipse in President's Park in front of the White House. Their pewter ornaments were so unique and beautiful that they have decorated the New Hampshire tree every year since.

Reproductions of these ornaments are now a part of Hampshire Pewter's catalog of more than 125 hand-crafted household items that are as beautiful as they are useful.

In a time when most pewter cups, mugs, and bowls are made from sheets of rolled pewter, Hampshire was founded in 1973 for the express purpose of reviving the methods that master pewterers have used for hundreds of years. They are the only company in the United States that uses the "Queen's Metal" formula for their work, and the only one certified to train master pewterers.

Their gleaming tableware, serving pieces, and gift sets add a rustic yet elegant dimension to any setting.

They also offer custom engraving services to make each gift more personal.

Their retail shop is at 9 Mill Street in Wolfeboro. During June to December they are open Monday through Saturday from 9:00 A.M. to 5:00 P.M.; January to May from 10:00 A.M. to 4:00 P.M. Also available at some finer jewelry, department, and gift stores—identified by Hampshire Pewter's distinctive "touch-mark" on each piece. Prices range from $4.00 to $175.00.

Catalog available for $2.00. Wholesale available. Products guaranteed. Price quotes on custom orders only, by letter. Shipped by either UPS or U.S. mail within six weeks. Will ship to Canada. Payment by MasterCard, Visa, check, or money orders.

Historic Hardware

Department NE
Box 1327
North Hampton, New Hampshire 03862
(603) 964-2280

Historic Hardware creates restoration quality hardware, lighting, and decorative accessories for any antique or reproduction home. Their specialties are thumblatch sets, strap hinges, and interior and exterior lighting fixtures. The craftspeople at Historic Hardware spend a lot of time researching and developing authentic reproductions.

The Suffolk thumblatch, first developed in the early 1700s, continued to be popular until the 1820s. Usually made by a local blacksmith, each latch was an expression of the artistry and craftsmanship of the maker. Each of Historic Hardware's Suffolk thumblatches are hand-forged.

The Norfolk thumblatch was introduced about 1800 and was one of the first latches to be made using machinery. It remained popular well into the twentieth century.

Most early lighting fixtures were simple and functuional, and Historic Hardware carries on that tradition by offering sconces, candle holders and light fixtures that are beautiful in their simplicity and functionality.

Historic Hardware also offers fireplace tools and accessories, hand-forged hinges, lanterns, hand-blown bull's eye glass for windows, and doorknockers in authentic colonial designs.

If detail is important to you, so is Historic Hardware.

Prices for the thumblatch sets range from $50.00 to $140.00. Sconces start at $18.00, and a four-arm chandelier is $225.00. Fireplace tools start at $19.00 with sets starting at $95.00. Doorknockers range from $24.00 to $65.00, and hinges from $80.00 to $150.00 per pair.

Historic Hardware operates a retail shop at 1000 Washington Road in Rye, New Hampshire, that is open Tuesday through Saturday from 9:00 A.M. to 5:00 P.M.

Catalog available for $3.00, refundable with purchase. Products guaranteed and can be returned except for special orders. Price quotes by letters or phone. Most goods stocked; some made to order. Goods shipped by UPS, unless otherwise requested, within eight weeks. Will ship to Canada. Payment by MasterCard, Visa, check, or money order.

Humane Trophies®/Dianne Shapiro Soft Sculpture, Inc.

19 Cedar Street
Brattleboro, Vermont 05301
(802) 254-8431

Humane Trophies® are a dramatic, warm-hearted group of soft-sculptured animals. Their special design, superior materials and workmanship capture the true nature of each animal and reveals its endearing characteristics.

These gentler versions of big game trophies are carefully handcrafted by a select group of Vermont artisans under the personal direction of Dianne Shapiro, designer and creator of Humane Trophies®.

Top quality acrylic furs and select fabrics are used to obtain the individual personality of each animal. The trophies are filled with 100 percent polyester, mounted on a plywood back, and ready to be easily mounted on a wall.

Originally inspired by the cartoonist Skip Morrow, the collection now includes 30 designs of the animals and their "other ends." It also includes the Bear Rug Collection: three 6' x 4 ½' critters that are excellent for floor and furniture decoration.

Humane Trophies® are a warm and humorous touch for decorating living rooms, dens, children's rooms, offices, professionals' waiting rooms, as well as restaurants, and other commercial locations. You can hunt the world over and not find anything quite like Humane Trophies®.

Catalog available for $3.00, refundable with purchase. Wholesale available. Products guaranteed. Goods stocked and shipped by UPS within two weeks. Will ship to Canada. Payment by MasterCard, Visa, check, or money order. A percentage of each sale is donated to wildlife organizations.

Bison	$96.00	Elephant	$160.00	Lion	76.00	Pig's Other End	60.00
Black Bear	52.00	Elephant's Other End	150.00	Lion's Other End	76.00	Polar Bear	52.00
Black Bear's Other End	76.00	Grizzly Bear	52.00	Moose	95.00	Polar Bear's	
Bull	96.00	Grizzly Bear's Other End	76.00	Moose's Other End	90.00	Other End	76.00
Cow	95.00	Hippopotamus	80.00	Oryx	96.00	Rhinoceros	80.00
Cow's Udder End	120.00	Horse's Other End	100.00	Panda	70.00	Sable Antelope	95.00
Deer	115.00	Jaguar	76.00	Panda's Other End	90.00	Zebra	90.00
Deer's Other End	70.00	Jaguar's Other End	76.00	Pig	52.00	Zebra's Other End	90.00

Kennedy Brothers

11 Main Street
Vergennes, Vermont 05491
(802) 877-2975

In the midst of the Great Depression, Paul and Jack Kennedy decided to invest in their own skills and pride of quality work. They founded Kennedy Brothers Woodenware, making shelves, toys, and home accessories.

Today, Kennedy Brothers has a larger work force, but they still maintain the pride in their work that inspired Paul and Jack to try it on their own. They make high quality wooden curio cabinets and shelves in different styles and patterns, and a wide selection of "Vermont Favorites" such as door harps, trivets, baskets, and birdfeeders. They also have special items for curio collectors including wood-base glass domes, plate stands, and spoon racks.

They handcraft each piece from the finest northern oak, pine, or black cherry, and give each item a water-resistant finish. Most cupboards feature adjustable shelving with plate grooves, and many have glass doors to protect fine collectibles.

Catalog available for $1.00. Wholesale available. Products guaranteed. Goods stocked are shipped by UPS or U. S. mail within six weeks. Larger items are shipped by truck. Will ship to Canada. Payment by MasterCard, Visa, or check.

Kennedy Brothers Woodenware is only one of more than 150 dealers who operate out of the Kennedy Brothers Factory Marketplace. Housed in an historic Vermont creamery building that has been restored with its double hung nine-over-nine windows, red brick walls, and open floor plan, the Factory Marketplace features more than 50 Vermont crafts outlets; 100 antique dealers; and such Vermont specialties as Ben and Jerry's Ice Cream Parlor, Beth's Bakery, The Owl's Basket Delicatessen, and the Vermont Artists Gallery. Located on Route 22A off U.S. Route 7 in Vergennes, it is open daily from 10:00 A.M. to 6:00 P.M.

Oak Colonnade Curio Cabinet 9037	$99.00
Clear View Curio Cabinet 9048	139.00
Corner Cupboard	109.00
"18-Cup" Cupboard	99.00
Vermont Butternut Tri-Stool	35.00
Vermont Express Wooden Train	36.00
Vermont Butternut Door Harp	26.00
Vermont Pie and Cake Basket	24.50

Kloter Farms

216 West Road
Ellington, Connecticut 06029
(800) 289-3463
(203) 871-1048

A gazebo adds a touch of elegance to any lawn or garden. Founded in 1980, Kloter Farms called on craftspeople with a penchant for detail to duplicate the gazebos of the nineteenth and early twentieth century using today's exacting engineering and construction techniques. This attention to detail and workmanship has paid off.

Throughout New England, the name Kloter Farms has become synonymous with handcrafted gazebos and quality storage buildings. They offer sizes and designs to fit every need.

If your small yard needs a touch of class, you might want to choose one of their models with an eight-foot diameter. Or you might be able to add a grand bit of elegance to a larger area by selecting a gazebo with an eighteen-foot diameter. They also offer models with ten, twelve, fourteen, and sixteen-foot diameters.

The *Imperial Classic,* with a steep roof pitch and graceful styling, is the most stately of the Kloter Farms gazebos .

The *Imperial* is similar to the *Imperial Classic*, but it has a lower roof profile, providing a less intrusive structure.

The *Pagoda* has a Far Eastern style with a distinctive roof design.

The *Marquise* is a ten-sided gazebo, blending style with extra usable space.

The *Imperial Pavillion* is a four-sided structure perfect for picnics or as an outdoor shelter.

The *Supreme* is their only model where western red cedar is standard, and provides the "do-it-yourselfer" with a project that combines superior materials and craftsmanship with a personal touch.

Kloter Farms handcrafts each individual gazebo as if they were going to use it themselves. They use custom-made modern trailers to deliver fully built storage buildings and gazebos where accessible, but they also ship them in disassembled sections anywhere in the world. Each piece is carefully wrapped in furniture pads to ensure its safety, and each comes with a step-by-step instructional video.

From the average backyard to the largest of town greens and corporate offices, a Kloter Farms gazebo will enhance any surrounding.

Prices range from $2,495.00 for an eight-foot Imperial to $5,775.00 for a 16-foot Imperial Classic. They also carry copper-top cupolas for $150.00 and built-in benches starting at $40.00.

Kloter Farms operates a retail outlet at 216 West Road (Route 83) in Ellington. It is New England's largest and most complete display of storage building, gazebos, and outdoor accessories. Call for hours.

Catalog available for $3.00, refundable with purchase. Wholesale available. Price quotes on custom orders only, by letter or phone. Some goods stocked; some made to order. Smaller items shipped UPS; buildings shipped by freight. Shipped within six weeks. Will ship to Canada. Payment by MasterCard, Visa, check, or money order.

"The elegance you deserve at a price you can afford."

Lorenzo Freccia Designs in Wood

8 Dexter Avenue
Seekonk, Massachusetts 02771
(508) 336-7520

Lorenzo Freccia specializes in making small wooden objects such as jewelry cases, cassette stands, small boxes, candleholders, and flower vases. His distinctive and original designs are handcrafted in solid domestic and exotic hardwoods and finished in oil to showcase the color and figure of the woods.

His lamps, compact disc stands, and menorahs display his superb workmanship. Simple, elegant lines are worked in cherry, ash, mahogany, walnut, maple, or padauk. Boxes that swivel on a central post or bowls that use a combination of woods for color patterns will complement both contemporary and traditional settings.

A cherry jewelry chest, for instance, has three layers. The top layer is a large compartment which sits on two tiers consisting of four swiveling drawers. His bud vase, on the other hand, is an urn-like design that is simple as well as elegant.

Free catalog. Wholesale available. Products guaranteed. Price quotes by letter or phone. Most goods are stocked; some made to order. Ships list items within six weeks; custom orders may take longer. Ships by UPS. Payment by MasterCard, Visa, check, or money order.

Cherry Jewelry Chest	$182.00
7-inch Lamp Base	130.00
Compact Disc Holder	82.00
Cassette Stand	68.00
Menorah	220.00
Group of Cherry Candleholders with connectors	38.00
Mahogany Bud Vase	16.00
Sweetheart Box	48.00
Moonlight Box	48.00

Maine Manna

P. O. Box 248
Gorham, Maine 04038
(207) 839-6013

For more than 20 years, Maine Manna has fed America's birds with top-grade kidney suet and a well-balanced mixture of bird seed. They never use cheaper filler seed, just sunflower seed, white millet, corn, peanut hearts, and thistle.

Of equal importance to the quality of the ingredients is the care that Maine Manna puts into producing its suet bird feed. The prime beef suet is heated in a special cooker to purge it of any bacteria, then mixed with the seed formula. Each container is individually filled and weighed to assure accuracy.

Because of their attention to detail, Maine Manna feeders have a shelf life of one year at room temperature. They will not turn rancid and fall apart, even during the summer. They even sell feeds to areas such as California and Florida throughout the entire year.

Their self-contained feeders start at $3.25, a great price to pay so that you can treat the songbirds in your area the year round.

Free catalog. Wholesale available. Price quotes by letter or phone. Products guaranteed. Goods stocked and shipped UPS or U.S. mail within one week. Will ship to Canada. Payment by MasterCard, Visa, or check.

13-ounce Feeders	$3.25
1.75-pound Feeders	4.50
1-pound Cakes	3.25
3.5-pound Cakes	8.00
6 7-ounce Cakes	10.00
Window Cake Feeder with two cakes	13.95
Handmade Holder for 1-pound cakes	7.50

Morse's Country Copper

P. O. Box 1220
Claremont, New Hampshire 03743
(603) 542-2324

In 1986 Donald Morse, a retired chemistry and biology teacher, began making copper windowsill trays for plants. These were so popular that Donald's family had to help him keep up with the demand. Before long, they discovered untapped artistic talent in their metal work, and although the windowsill trays are still their best selling item, they have branched out in several directions.

The Morses specialize in a copper art that is functional as well as beautiful. Their light fixtures, lanterns, servingware, dishes, and household accessories add a touch of American heritage to any home. They also offer a line of copper weathervanes that are individually constructed by hand either as a silhouette figure or full-bodied. The directional letters are cast in bronze and they offer an unique adjustable roof mount for each weathervane. The Morses also produce custom work.

Prices for the weathervanes range from $125.00 to $1490.00. Other products ranges from $8.00 for a crimped heart candle holder to $175.00 for a petal chandelier.

The Morses operate a retail shop in Unity Center, New Hampshire. They are open Monday through Saturday from 9:00 A.M. to 5:00 P.M.

Free catalog. Wholesale available. Price quotes by letter or phone. Most goods are stocked; some made to order. Products guaranteed. Shipped UPS within two weeks. Will ship to Canada. Payment by check.

New England Woodturners

P. O. Box 7242
75 Daggett Street
New Haven, Connecticut 06519
(203) 776-1880

Ⓝ ew England Woodturners has a reputation as the finest woodturning studio in New England. They can make any turned piece of wood from a chess piece to a 40-foot column, from one piece to thousands. Their duplicating lathe provides excellent reproduction detail on jobs requiring a large number of pieces, and their specialties include balusters, newels, Victorian porch posts, and custom columns. All work is hand turned and hand sanded in both directions, and suitable for paint or staining.

They also provide design consultation and problem solving. Although they primarily work with architects, builders, cabinetmakers, and restoration contractors, they also work directly with many homeowners.

Out of this work, New England Woodturners has received an overwhelming number of requests for a production series baluster. They have responded by designing a line of balusters featuring traditional style and grace. The five styles of their Signature Series Balusters are Guildford, Boston, Tulip, Hartford, and Old Haven. In addition to the standard 32-, 34-, and 36-inch lengths, they will turn any size up to 54 inches.

A free brochure is available, but since all work is custom made, prices must be quoted. Prices depend on item ordered, size, quantity, and kind of wood used. Be sure to provide as much information as possible so that an accurate quotation may be made. Products guaranteed. Ships UPS or common carrier within eight weeks. Will ship to Canada. Payment by check or money order.

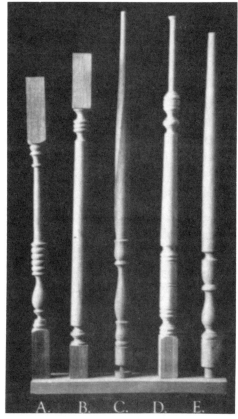

Signature Series Balusters: A. Guilford; B. Boston; C. Tulip; D. Hartford; E. Old Haven

NEW ENGLAND
WOODTURNERS

North Country Wind Bells

Box 127
Round Pond, Maine 04564
(207) 677-2224

As the cool fog rolls over the harbor, the gentle tones of the buoy bells echo across the water, guiding travelers and adding a dreamy sound to life on the harbor.

Determined to capture these enchanting sounds, Jim Davidson recorded actual buoy bells. Then using Cor-Ten steel, a low-maintenance metal manufactured by U. S. Steel, Jim painstakingly cut the metal until the tones of his North Country Wind Bells carried the sounds of the harbor buoys.

He continued to work with the steel, the tapes, and his memory until he was satisfied that the Nantucket Bell, the Pemaquid Bell, the Bar Harbor Bell, and the Boothbay Harbor Bell reflected his interpretation of several of the bell buoys in each of the areas for which the bells are named. He completed his set of wind bells by adding an Island Pasture Bell.

Maine Buoy Bells are designed to hang outdoors year round. As they weather, they turn a rich rust color which preserves and improves the tones through the years.

Fine quality American-made materials and pride in workmanship mean that these rugged chimes from North Country Wind Bells will endure to the point of

becoming family heirlooms. Each bell is packed with a card containing information about the history and artisanry of the bells.

Jim also handcrafts Maine Scare Cats to guard your home or garden, and scroll hangers for the windbells.

Prices of the windbells range from $22.00 for the Island Pasture Bell to $52.00 for the Nantucket Buoy Bell. The Maine Scare Cat is $18.00, and the scroll hangers range from $8.00 to $10.00.

Free catalog. Wholesale available. Products guaranteed. Goods stocked and shipped U. S. mail within two weeks. Will ship to Canada. Payment by American Express, MasterCard, Visa, check, or money order.

Prints and Patches

Main Street
P. O. Box 1205
Stowe, Vermont 05672
(802) 253-8643

Many people who would like to have a quilt do not have the time, energy, or knowledge to make one. Prints and Patches can solve this problem.

You design the quilt. Choose one of the nine patterns and the color combination. Prints and Patches custom makes the quilt for you, double stitching each seam for strength and using only machine washable fabrics for easy care.

Prints and Patches also offers pillows, wallhangings, quilted jackets (children's and adult sizes), children's pinafores and aprons, baby quilts and buntings, shams and dust ruffles, Christmas tree skirts and Christmas stockings.

Prints and Patches operates a retail shop on site, open Monday through Saturday from 10:00 A.M. to 5:00 P.M.

Free catalog. Price quotes by letter or phone. Products guaranteed. Materials for the quilts are stocked. Quilts are made and shipped within 12 weeks by UPS, U.S. mail. Will ship to Canada. Payment by American Express, MasterCard, Visa, check, or money order.

Pattern Choices	Twin	Double/Queen	King
Starburst	$287.00	$277.00	$307.00
Double Wedding Ring	407.00	607.00	707.00
Stenciled Basket	387.00	457.00	507.00
Log Cabin	287.00	337.00	397.00
Sundance	287.00	337.00	397.00
Hearts Delight	387.00	457.00	507.00
Ohio Star	287.00	337.00	397.00
Trip Around the World	237.00	277.00	307.00
Appliquéd Vermont Landscape	387.00	457.00	507.00

Color Choices		
Navy	Peach	Navy/Mauve
Peach/Blue	Slate Blue	Slate Blue/Rose
Lilac/Purple	Forest Green	Rose/Burgundy
Red	Yellow	Soft Green/Peach
Earth Tones	Soft Green	

Royalston Oak

North Fitzwilliam Road
Royalston, Massachusetts 01368
(508) 249-9633

Royalston Oak believes there is more to building a new home than choosing between conventional construction and high-priced custom housing, and that quality is not just a function of price or name.

Royalston Oak specializes in building timber frames for houses, barns, and house additions in oak, pine, and hemlock. They will travel anywhere in New England to raise a timber frame. They also offer design services and encourage the use of skin panel enclosure systems as well as some hard-to-find products that will complement your timber frame project.

Royalston Oak has been creating authentic handmade timber frame homes since 1977. The timbers for each frame are finished in their shops and assembled on your foundation along with a superinsulated envelope system. The house can then be completed using your own selections of doors, windows, siding, etc.

Tom Musco, founder of the company and master timber framer, has a degree in sculpture and began his professional woodworking career as a musical instrument maker. He has tried to use his sculptural sense and the precision craftsmanship required for building

Phillipston Cape, 1498 sq. ft.

musical intruments to produce timber frames of the highest quality and beauty.

Tom and the other craftspeople at Royalston Oak are determined to make living in a timber frame house like living in a finely sculpted piece of furniture. Owning a Royalston Oak home means having a home of constructed with an innovative design and uncompromising attention to workmanship and detail.

Prices for the timber frames vary greatly. Depending on the location, complexity, size, location and finish details, the cost usually ranges from $10.00 to $12.00 per square foot. The cost for the enclosure system generally ranges from $4.25 to $4.50 per square foot of house surface area.

Catalog available for $5.00. Products guaranteed. Price quotes by letter or phone. Goods are made to order. Shipped by truck within 24 weeks. Payment by check.

Dana Saltbox, 1470 sq. ft.

ROYALSTON OAK

Rue de France

78 Thames Street
Newport, Rhode Island 02840
(401) 846-2084
(800) 777-0998 (for orders)

Several years ago, when Pamela Kelley and her husband were living in Paris, France, she fell in love with the beautiful country lace curtains she saw in one of the oldest sections of the city. With her husband's help, Pamela founded Rue de France, the only American company importing the country lace of France to America.

Since the seventeenth century French country lace from LePuy, Chantilly, Caudry, and Calais has been the standard when judging the quality of fine lace. Today, French artisans, many from families that have been making lace for more than 200 years, produce the same beautiful country designs as their ancestors, using the same kind of looms and machines used during the time of Napoleon.

Pamela and her staff import this lace to make beautiful curtains and tablecloths, placemats and pillows. They feature more than fifteen designs, and will custom-fit any window's measurements. They also offer decorator accessories and all the hardware needed to hang the curtains.

Rue de France operates a retail shop at 78 Thames Street in Newport, open Monday through Saturday from 10:00 A.M. to 6:00 P.M. and Sunday from 12:00 P.M. to 5:00 P.M.

Catalog available for $3.00. Wholesale is available. Price quotes by letter or phone. Product shipped by UPS or U.S. Mail within three weeks. Will ship to Canada. Payment by American Express, MasterCard, Visa, check, or money order.

Pattern	Width	Length	Price
Etoile Sheer Panels	72"	45" or 54"	$76.00
Panier Flat Panels	23"	36" or 40"	33.00
Belle Fleur Flat Panels	23"	45" or 54"	36.00
Papillon Valance	44"	12"	35.00
Doves Tiebacks (Pair)	70"	54"	90.00
La Jardin Tablecloth	60"	80"	68.00
Rose Lace Tablerunner	17"	54"	34.00

Russ Loomis, Jr., Fine Furniture and Cabinetmaker

R219 B
Williamsburg, Massachusetts 01096
(413) 628-3813

Since 1974, Russ Loomis, Jr., has been making furniture, working with a wide variety of styles, although his preference is for Queen Anne and Chippendale.

Instead of making exact repoductions of antiques, however, Russ hand-crafts original pieces that are in keeping with the style of a particular period. Each piece is individually designed and made using only the very finest materials and techniques. He makes tables, desks, lowboys, highboys, chests, chairs, beds, and more. Most of his furniture is one-of-a-kind, and he is continually trying new variations to give more variety to a standard style.

Russ uses woods that are carefully selected for each piece, and a hand-rubbed finish highlights the unique beauty of the grain. His joinery is painstakingly crafted, and his signature on his work assures you that each piece is one-of-a-kind and is always of heirloom quality.

Catalog available for $3.00, refundable with purchase. Products guaranteed. All items are made to order. Price quotes by letter or phone. Shipped by truck. Shipping time varies according to item ordered. Will ship to Canada. Payment by check or money order.

Russ Loomis, Jr.
fine furniture & cabinetmaker

Queen Anne Mirror	$ 500.00
Queen Anne Tea Table	1,000.00
Hepplewhite Dining Table	3,500.00
Chippendale Chest of Drawers	4,000.00
Chippendale Armoire	5,000.00

Shelter-Kit Incorporated

22 Mill Street
P. O. Box 1
Tilton, New Hampshire 03276
(603) 934-4327

Since 1970 Shelter-Kit Incorporated has been producing high quality, pre-cut buildings in kit form. From a selection of small cabins designed for remote locations to homes, garages, and barns, Shelter-Kit has the building you want for a price you can afford.

Each kit comes with easy step-by-step instructions and precision-cut materials. No carpentry skills are needed. Lumber is pre-sawn and pre-drilled to minute tolerances, so only hand tools are needed for assemble. The kits come with all materials so you don't have to make countless trips to the lumberyard for one more two-by-four or another pound of nails.

A complete, illustrated construction manual is sent ahead of the materials for familiarization with assembly procedures. Materials are packaged in clearly marked, approximately 100-pound bundles for easy portability.

Each house kit, with its unique post-and-beam framing system, is ready for expansion. Buy what you can afford now and add on as time and finances allow.

The 24' x 24' Barn Kit is $8,000.00. The 20' x 20' Garage kit is $4,745.00. House kits range from $4,750.00 to $25,610.00.

Retail store on site, open Monday through Friday from 8:30 A.M. to 4:30 P.M. and on weekends by appointment.

Catalog available for $6.00. Price quotes by letter or phone. Products guaranteed. Catalogs shipped by UPS or U.S. mail within one week. Buildings are shipped by motor freight within six weeks. Payment by MasterCard, Visa, check, or money order.

Two-bedroom Lofthouse

Stoneham Pewter

RFD #1, Box 14421
Stoneham Corners
Brookfield, New Hampshire 03872
(603) 522-3425

T ed and Cheryl White have been making fine, gravity-cast, hand-turned pewter since they started Stoneham Pewter in 1979. Each piece produced is an original design and is signed and dated by Cheryl to authenticate it.

Stoneham pewter is made of lead-free pewter consisting of 92 percent tin, with copper and antimony added in proportions equivalent to fine British pewter of the early eighteenth century.

They specialize in oil lamps, candleholders, napkin rings, bells, goblets, even cordials.

Oil Lamps

Prices range from $10.00 to $125.00 each. Call or write for more information. Goods stocked and shipped UPS. Payment by MasterCard, Visa, check, or money order.

Stuart • Townsend • Carr

P. O. Box 373
Limington, Maine 04049
(207) 793-4522
(800) 637-2344

During the nineteenth century, a classic bookcase design was popular with the students at Harvard and other universities. Made of five graduated shelf units with end handholds that rest on a four-drawer base, the bookcase could also be used to carry clothes and books to college. Over the years, "Harvard Bookcase" became a generic term to describe this flexible and practical piece of furniture.

Today, Stuart • Townsend • Carr makes reproductions of this and other classics. With years of experience in architectural woodworking, furniture making, and antiques restoration, they once specialized in one-of-a-kind custom orders, from Palladian windows to circular stairs, from custom furniture to precise copies of period antiques. They found a strong demand for a range of furniture forms, high in quality and design, that is unavailable elsewhere. They offer desks, credenzas, tables, "office butlers," as well as compact disc and video cassette racks.

In addition to the Harvard Bookcase, they offer a Revolving Bookcase—one of America's true national styles—a credenza with a hidden shelf for a computer keyboard, and other elegant designs for office or home.

Each piece has their guarantee of workmanship and customer satisfaction. It must include great design, proven function, solid woods, dove-tailed or mortised joints, and multiple-step hand finishing using the best materials.

Catalog available for $4.00. Products guaranteed. Price quotes by letter or phone. Items shipped by UPS or truck within eight weeks of purchase. Payment by American Express, MasterCard, Visa, check, or money order.

Standard 4-shelf Revolving Bookcase	$1,175.00
Record Album 2-shelf Revolving Bookcase	1,075.00
Compact Disk 4-shelf Revolving Rack	375.00
Video Cassette 5-shelf Revolving Rack	850.00
Coffee Table with Glass Top Display Box	485.00
Writing Desk	875.00
Library Modular Unit	850.00
Standard Harvard Bookcase	2,250.00
Office Butler	2,250.00
Credenza	2,250.00
Panel Desk	4,800.00

Sturbridge Studio

114 East Hill
Brimfield, Massachusetts 10101
(413) 245-3289

Sturbridge Studio is a group of artists who can turn your favorite photograph into enduring art. Initially, they were inspired by a love of the fine old buildings and landscapes of New England. Now they are turning their attention to homes and gardens.

Sturbridge Studio can turn your snapshot into a beautifully rendered pen and ink drawing. They enjoy working from both present day photographs and from old pictures.

Just call or write Sturbridge for a free brochure and order form, then choose your favorite photograph or slide in color or black and white. Photos may be an exterior or interior of a home, garden, or landscape.

Sturbridge offers three standard sizes for the drawings: 5" x 7", 11" x 14", and 20" x 24". All drawings are finished with a high grade, bevel-edge mat. There are six colors of mats to choose from, and all drawings are completed in black ink. Special sizes and mat colors are available. A framing service is available on request for an additional charge.

Approximately eight weeks will be needed for completion of the drawing. All work is submitted for approval on completion. If for some reason, you do not like the completed drawing, the full price, less a 10% deposit will be cheerfully refunded.

Prices for the drawings are $80.00 for a 5" x 7" (matted 8" x 10"), $125.00 for an 11" x 14" (matted 20" x 24"), and $275.00 for a 20" x 24" (matted 24" x 32").

Drawings are shipped UPS or U.S. mail depending on customer preference. Payment by check or money order.

U. S. Bells

P. O. Box 73
Prospect Harbor, Maine 04669
(207) 963-7184

In 1970 Richard Fisher was working with metal sculpture when he became intrigued with the idea of an art form that combined wind, motion, and sound. He first experimented with sheet steel, then cast bronze.

He now makes a selection of handmade wind and doorbells with a pleasing range of tones that change with the weather, so that the tones heard on a bright

sunny day are different from those when the weather is cold and rainy.

Richard's first experimental bells fascinated his customers with their smooth round design and a clapper that hung outside the bell. The bronze does not rust. An aging bell develops a mellow patina without changing the clear sound of the bell.

Richard continues to experiment, making improvements in his foundry and designs, but his unique porch and doorbells, mobiles, dinner bells, tea bells, and chimes already make for charming, distinctive complements to any home.

U. S. Bells has a retail store on Route 186 in Prospect Harbor. The store is open Monday through

Friday from 8:00 A.M. to 4:00 P.M. Retail prices range from $27.00 to $295.00. Bells are available in some craft galleries and gift and specialty shops.

Free catalog. Products guaranteed. Wholesale available. Price quotes by letter or phone. Goods usually stocked and shipped by UPS within three weeks. Will ship to Canada. Payment by MasterCard, Visa, check, or money order.

Van Engelen, Inc.

Stillbrook Farm
313 Maple Street
Litchfield, Connecticut 06759
(203) 567-8734
(203) 567-5662

Crocuses and daffodils are our first harbingers of spring, often blooming even while snow is still in the air. Tulips and irises are traditional beauties that add a touch of elegance to any home or garden. The Moonlight Lily blooms late in the summer, lending a bit of magic to hot, lazy days.

Jan S. Ohms, president of Van Engelen, is the fourth generation in his family to develop and sell bulb flowers. Van Engelen offers more than 400 varieties of bulbs, most of which are shipped from the family nursery in Holland. They sell only the finest bulbs available at the lowest possible prices.

Bulbs for individual flowers are packed and priced per hundred. One pack of the Black Forest Tulip, for example, contains 100 bulbs for $24.50. The Anne Frank Tulip is $26.50 per hundred, and the Narcissi Grand Mixture, which includes several varieties of narcissi, is $39.75.

Van Engelen Inc.

Van Engelen also offers a selection of bulb collections containing 50 bulbs of six varieties of similar flowers such as May-Flowering tulips or Darwin Hybrid tulips. These collections start at around $75.00.

Call or write Van Engelen for a free catalog.

Wholesale available. Price quotes on orders of more than 5,000 bulbs, by letter or phone. Minimum order of $50.00. Bulbs shipped after September 15. Ships UPS. Payment by MasterCard, Visa, check, or money order.

Kaufmania Hybrids

Crocus and Narcissi
Novelties

Hyacinths

Vermont Country Pine Products

P. O. Box 538
Swanton, Vermont 05488
(802) 868-3511

Located deep in the heart of the Green Mountains, Vermont Country Pine Products provides their customers with a unique collection of beautiful Americana pieces crafted to add a special warmth to any room.

It all started with a quaint little Shaker rack decorated with a model of a small Vermont town. It was the first item they offered nationally, and it is still one of their best sellers. It was such a success that they began to expand their line, and now offer more than 100 items.

Items such as their calico cats with long tails and curious expressions are perfect for a window or narrow shelf. Or try their north country sleigh bench, a unique New England design. Their seven-piece miniature New England village is a decorative touch for any room and just right for sitting on one of Aunt Lu's kitchen shelves—a handmade utility shelf based on a Shaker design.

At prices that start at less than $10.00, you'll find it easy to add a bit of personality and charm to your home with early American touches such as butter churns, wash benches, pouting chairs, hardwood candlesticks, cupboards, wagons, magazine racks, and all manner of decorative accessories. Vermont Country Pine Products can bring a little of Vermont into your home, and help create a country lifestyle that is unique.

Catalog subscription available for $2.00. Products guaranteed. Goods stocked and shipped by UPS. Payment by American Express, MasterCard, Visa, check, or money order.

Whaler Boy Wall Plaque	$24.00
Morgan Hobby Horse	12.00
The Green Mountain Express	75.00
Country Wash Bench Checkerboard	50.00
Handpainted Christmas Village	115.00
Victorian Country Clock	36.00
Door Harp	38.00
Boston Colonial Shelf	35.00
Shaker Rack	34.00
Garden Basket	24.00
Wire Egg Basket	11.00
Hiding Ironing Board	95.00
Metal Tricycle	45.00
Cow Doorstop	16.00
2-pound brick Sharp Cheddar	13.00
8-ounce jar Apple Butter	4.00
"Northern Comfort" Maple Syrup	14.00

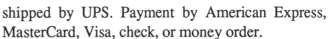

Vermont Wildflower Farm

Route 7
Charlotte, Vermont 05445
(802) 425-3931

The Vermont Wildflower Farm is the largest wildflower seed company in the East, offering high-quality mixtures specially created and hand packed for each region of North America. Wildflowers are simple to plant and easy to grow. All you need is a plot of ground or a windowbox and the right seeds.

Their mixture for the "The Historic Northeast" features flaming red poppies, sky-blue cornflowers, white drifts of wild baby's breath, yellow coreopsis, and pink, white, and gold wild cosmos.

"America's Heartland" includes black-eyed susans, gloriosa daisies, purple prairie coneflowers, deep pink dame's rocket, and bright yellow lance-leaf coreopsis.

Wild baby's breath, gaillardia, scarlet flax, red poppy, and yellow/maroon coreopsis are part of the mix for "The Sunny South." "The Wild, Wild West" features seeds for lupine, Indian blanket, wild cosmos, daisies, and purple and yellow coneflowers.

Their mixture for "The Southwest and Southern California" features Chinese houses, globe gilia, lupine, desert bluebell, rose mallow, blue flax, and twenty-six other species. "The Pacific Northwest and Northern California" includes seeds for wild foxglove, red flax, wild shasta daisy and golden lupine.

Prices for all mixtures range from $7.95 for one ounce (which covers up to 250 square feet) to $375.00 for a ten-pound bag that plants 43,000 square feet, and includes a free copy of *The Wildflower Meadow Book.*

The Vermont Wildflower Farm also offers packets of individual species such as daisies, red poppies, black-eyed susans, and more. The individual packets come in a variety of sizes, with small packets starting at $1.25.

Their catalog includes other gift items such as books, wreaths, wildflower vases, potpourri, and guides to all types of wildflowers.

Their retail shop sits amid six acres of wildflower test fields on Route 7 in Charlotte. It is open daily from May 1 through mid-October. Hours are from 10:00 A.M. to 5:00 P.M.

Free catalog. Wholesale available. Minimum order is $7.00. Price quotes for large landscape orders only, by letter or phone. Products guaranteed. Goods are stocked and shipped within two weeks by UPS or U.S. mail. Special mixes for Canada. Payment by American Express, MasterCard, Visa, check, or money order.

Western Maine Cedar Products

School Street
P. O. Box 445
Stockton Springs, Maine 04981
800-448-5567

Northern white cedar is one of the strongest, most durable woods known. It is insect resistant and stands up in the worst weather conditions, making it perfect for outdoor items such as planters and bird-feeders.

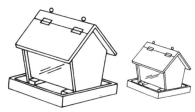

Western Maine Cedar Products specializes in home and garden accessories made from northern white cedar. Each item is joined with galvanized nails, and shipped completely assembled for immediate use. The bird houses also come with bird identification tips, consumer tip tags, and placement suggestions.

The planters come in sizes ranging from a 13" x 5½" herb planter to a 19" x 19" V-matched patio planter. The versatile flower boxes add a distinctive touch to any area. The trellises will give climbing plants a place to grow for years to come.

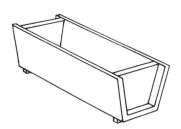

Western Maine Cedar's Garden Mates make carrying fruits, vegetables, and seeding flats easy instead of a burden. Sturdy but lightweight, the Garden Mates come in three sizes: Small (20" x 8" x 2"), Large (20" x 14" x 2"), and Large-Deep (20" x 14" x 4").

Free catalog. Wholesale available. Products guaranteed. Price quotes for quantity and special orders only, by phone or letter. Will do custom work. Other goods stocked and shipped within three weeks by UPS or motor freight. Will ship to Canada. Payment by MasterCard or Visa.

Oh, yes, they also sell bat houses. For real bats. Since the number of natural roosting places for bats has diminished, bat houses provide a cozy home for these insect-eating friends.

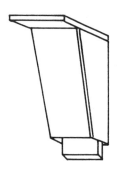

Walpole Woodworkers

767 East Street
Walpole, Massachusetts 02081
(800) 343-6948 (outside Massachusetts)
(617) 668-2800 (Massachusetts, Alaska, Hawaii)

Walpole Woodworkers makes classic fences that withstand the rigors of time and changing styles. Researching and preparing hundreds of original and historic designs enables Walpole to sell fences that blend with the natural landscape as well as offering privacy and a bit of elegance.

Walpole fencing begins with a careful selection of northern white cedar that is cut by Walpole in its own mill specifically for the fence design that you have chosen for your home.

A rustic fence matches the trees around it, and Walpole offers several of these styles, including a Salem or Colonial spaced picket with slender vertical line or a Rustic Virgina fence with diagonal pales.

A Square-Edged fence is symmetrical with clean lines and perfect balance. Popularized during the Victorian era, it can be as simple or elaborate as you wish.

A Screen fence offers more privacy as well as being one of the most versatile and beautiful fences.

The Picket fence reflects a 200-year-old tradition of simplicity and practicality and can be designed to have simple lines and tops or with design flourishes that will set any house apart.

Now licensed to reproduce the distinctive fences and gates of Williamsburg, Virginia, Walpole can make your home a contemporary showplace or an historic recreation with such fences as a George Wythe picket with its intricate pales and flame-shaped tops, or a William Prentis fence with its diamond-top pales.

Yorktown Capper Five-foot Chestnut Fence

In addition, Walpole Woodworkers offers a wide selection of small buildings, and rustic furniture, including chairs, tables, chaises, settees, serving carts, stools, benches, and swings. They also carry home accessories, such as lanterns, mailbox posts, flag poles, weathervanes and children's playsets.

Walpole Woodworkers operates several retail shops around the country, but will ship their materials anywhere.

Catalog available for $6.00. Products guaranteed, except for items damaged by the customer during assembly. Goods are stocked and shipped UPS or motor freight. Will ship to Canada. Payment by American Express, MasterCard, Visa, check, or money order.

Clockwise: Boothbay Rocker, Penobscot Settee,
Kennebec Arm Chair, Pocasset Table

White Flower Farm

Litchfield, Connecticut 06759-0050
(800) 888-7756
(203) 496-1418 (FAX)

White Flower Farm serves more than 200,000 gardeners around the country, and their attention to quality has secured them certificates of excellence from the American Horticultural Society and the Federated Garden Clubs of Connecticut.

They produce three catalogs a year, each filled with beautiful photography and interesting horticultural information about their plants. From rare plant bulbs to fully grown hanging baskets of "Strawberry Firetails," from plants for your office to wreaths for your door, White Flower will handle any challenge. And this is the place to order the famed Tellicherry peppercorns and topiary rosemary plants. They also offer copper planters, terracotta bowls, gardening stools and magazines. If you still aren't sure what to buy for that special gardener in your life, White Flower will provides a gift certificate for the occasion.

Catalog subscription available for $5.00, which includes three issues. Subscription is refundable with purchase. Products guaranteed. Plants shipped UPS or Federal Express. Shipping time varies. Payment by American Express, MasterCard, Visa, check, or money order.

Acalypha "Strawberry Firetails" Hanging Basket	$32.00
Potted Hyacinths	23.00
Flowering Hibiscus	26.00
1-pound bag Tellicherry Black Peppercorns	14.00
8-inch Terra Cotta Bulb Bowl	15.00
Topiary Rosemary	30.00
Clivia in Terra Rossa Pot	56.00
Gardening Stool	56.00
Beginning Rose Garden	45.00
A Pot of Freesias	42.00
Herb Wreath	55.00
Jasmine Hanging Basket	30.00

Wood Ware

Box 1268
RD 4, Rt 7 South
Middlebury, Vermont 05753
802-388-6297

In 1983 a visitor to Charles Herrmann's shop became enchanted with the door harps that play a musical phrase each time a door is opened or closed. They are unusual instruments that are made of butternut wood and are Swedish in origin.

The Herrmanns sell hundreds of handmade wooden items at their shop and by mail. Duck decoys, lawn chairs and tables, home decorations—each with the quality that marks them as "Made in Vermont." But the door harps are one of the most popular items, and Charles Herrmann sells more than a thousand each year. The handcarved and handpainted harps add a bit of entrancing hospitality to any home.

Who was that enchanted visitor from 1983? It was bestselling author Chaim Potok, who used one of the Herrmann's harps as the central motif in his novel, *Davita's Harp*.

Retail outlet on site. Call for hours.

Free catalog. Wholesale available. Goods stocked and shipped UPS or U.S. mail within 12 days. Will ship to Canada. Payment by check or money order.

Large Heart Cutout Doorharp	$26.95
Large Handpainted Lyre Shape Doorharp	29.50
Small Covered Bridge Doorharp	9.95
Cedar Goose	29.85
10-inch Hardwood Sanded Bowl	4.95
Folding Maple Chair	49.95
Folding Maple Rocker	59.95
Adirondack Lawn Chair Kit	39.95
Catskill Mountain Windchimes	49.95
White Cedar Swing Set	195.00

Woodbury's Woodenware

Box 303
Shelburne, Vermont 05482
(802) 985-3742

I n 1941, Glenn Woodbury started making hand-turned bowls in the basement of his home. Word of the quality and artistry of his work spread, and Glenn opened a shop. Visitors carried news of his work all over the country. Today, the heirloom quality of Woodbury Woodenware is available in more than 400 shops coast-to-coast, at their factory outlet in Shelburne, and by mail order direct from their factory.

Properly cared for, Woodbury's products can last for generations. All products are made from kiln-dried Vermont yellow birch, shaped by hand on a face-plate lathe, and carefully sealed from any moisture. Salad bowls, lazy susans, serving bowls, and ice buckets are among Woodbury's select items.

The line of trivets and cheese trays are made even more distinctive by the use of hand painted tiles. Designed and painted by Jeanne Haskell, the tiles highlight the birds and wildflowers of New England. Most products are under $50.00.

Woodbury's operates a retail shop on Route 7 in Shelburne, across from the Shelburne Museum.

Free catalog. Wholesale available. Price quotes for unique items only, by phone. Some goods are stocked; some made-to-order. Shipped by UPS or U.S. mail with delivery within four weeks. Will ship to Canada. Payment by MasterCard, Visa, or check.

Tile Designs		
Iris	Chidee	Fiddlehead
Orchid	Trout Lily	Cardinal
Blue Sunflower	Violet	Loon
Gold Sunflower	Trillium	Day Lily
Bluebell	Thrush	Pond Lily
Gold Bluebell	Canada Goose	Yellow Lady Slipper
Hummingbird	Pink Lady Slipper	

Stephen Zeh ♦ Basketmaker

P. O. Box 381M
Temple, Maine 04984
(207) 778-2351

As a professional trapper, Stephen Zeh found that the baskets he bought to carry his traps were badly made and fell apart quickly. He decided to make his own.

First, he visited Eddie Newell, a Penobscot Indian basketmaker who taught Stephen that "quality takes time." Stephen learned how to handcraft each basket

in the manner of the Maine Shakers, woodsmen, and Native American basketmakers. Next, he started looking for the right tree.

Stephen uses only Maine brown ash wood for his baskets. The brown ash is a rare tree that grows mostly in swampland, and only one in a hundred makes a good basket tree. He then pounds the wood until the growth rings separate into thin, strong, lightweight strips, which he scrapes by hand to a smooth satin finish. He uses 15 to 25 trees a year and can only get 75 to 100 splints from each tree. He handcarves the basket rims and handles along the grain of the wood, then bends them slowly with his hands and knees.

Quality takes time, but it also has its rewards. Stephen's baskets have been in juried shows at the Smithsonian and the Philadelphia Museum of Art. His baskets have been displayed at Hancock Shaker Village, and on the cover of *Vogue Knitting International*. Stephen advertises his baskets in *Down East* and the *New Yorker*, and his baskets have been called the finest ever made. Edgar Allen Beem of the *Maine Times* said of Stephen's baskets, "You'll pay over ten times as much for a Stephen Zeh basket as you will for most splint ash baskets, but you'll get what you pay for."

Catalog available for $2.00. Baskets range in price from $85.00 to $1200.00. Wholesale is available to select shops, galleries and interior designers. Baskets are made to order and shipped by UPS within 16 weeks. Payment by MasterCard, Visa, check, or money order.

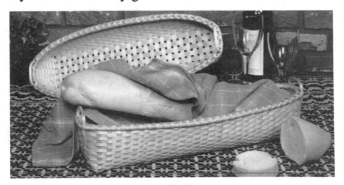

PUTTING ON THE RITZ

NEW ENGLAND CRAFTED CLOTHING AND PERSONAL ACCESSORIES

Fall River Knitting Mills

P. O. Box 995
Flint Station
Fall River, Massachusetts 02723-0995
(800) 446-1089

In 1911, Frank Reitzas had a dream. He worked 14-hour days as a knitter in New York City, but he wanted to run his own business. Finally scraping together $50.00, he bought a knitting machine. He worked nights, and his wife, Flora, sold his fabric during the day. Fall River Knitting Mills was born.

The family still runs the business, still operating under Frank's belief that "the best doesn't have to be expensive. Give them the best and let them go home with some change in their pockets." They take pride in the quality as well as the price of their garments.

They use only the finest cotton and woolen yarns for their knits, and every step of the making and mailing of their garments is handled right in their mill, eliminating the complicated manufacturing and distribution process that causes other companies to maintain higher prices. By relying on an expert staff and quality fabric, they make sure they take care of their most valued asset: their customer.

Visitors to Fall River can visit the historic mill that houses the company, and customers can save up to 50 percent in any of their regional outlets, which carry their full line of clothes, from Shetland and turtleneck sweaters to polo shirts and sun dresses. Prices for sweaters start at $15.00.

Free catalog. Wholesale available. No price quotes. Goods stocked and shipped by UPS or U.S. mail within three weeks. Products guaranteed. Payment by MasterCard, Visa, Discover, check, or money order.

Retail Outlets

All outlets open seven days a week. Please call for times.

69 Alden St.	Roue 28/Iyanough Rd.	16-18 Main St.	Route 4
Fall River, MA	Hyannis, MA	Plymouth, MA	Quechee, VT
508-678-7553	508-775-2037	508-747-2037	802-295-7920
Main St.	192-194 Thames St.	Route 1, Exit 2 off I-95	
North Conway, NH	Newport, RI	Wells, ME	
603-356-3970	401-849-5209	207-646-9641	

J. H. Breakell and Company

69 Mill Street
Newport, Rhode Island 02840
(800) 767-6411
(401) 849-3522

When James Breakell started silversmithing in 1972, he created a line of fine jewelry and holloware that was both beautiful and unique. Since each design is copyrighted and each item carefully handcrafted, every piece of Breakell jewelry is an example of the high quality that Jim insists on having in his work. By giving his personal guarantee for quality and customer satisfaction, and by advertising in such publications as *The New Yorker* and *Smithsonian*, Jim has slowly increased his mail order business, and now offers the work of other New England craftspeople as well as his own.

Many of the ideas for Jim's work come from nature. His Victory Garden collection, for example, includes fourteen karat gold and sterling silver pendants and brooches shaped like vegetables. The Breakell dedication to traditional workmanship is evident in the intricate detail of each piece whether it is a simple mushroom or a more complicated ear of corn. The other vegetables in his Victory Garden are artichokes, peas, leeks, stalks of asparagus and broccoli.

Other pieces include earrings, brooches, bangles, and pendants that portray whales, dolphins, seagulls, and shells. His luxurious hand-hammered cuff bracelets can be purchased plain or with individual hand engraving. Other artistic and unusual designs are aimed at appealing to almost every taste.

The 16-page free color catalog of the J. H. Breakell line is mailed twice a year. Jim also maintains a retail store at 69 Mill Street in Newport, which is open Monday through Saturday from 9:00 A.M.-5:00 P.M.

Price quotes by letter are available only for custom work. Other goods are stocked and shipped UPS and U.S. mail within four weeks. Will ship to Canada. Payment by American Express, MasterCard, Visa, check, or money order.

	Sterling Silver	*14-Karat Gold*
Mushroom	$35.00	$458.00
Corn Pin	30.00	280.00
Artichoke Brooch	35.00	418.00
Broccoli Brooch	35.00	376.00
Leek Pin	35.00	300.00
Tomato Pin	35.00	448.00

Lepeltier Corporation

Box 61
East Fairfield, Vermont 05448
(802) 827-3840

For more than four centuries, clay pipes have been cherished throughout Europe for their faithful interpretation of tobacco flavor. Even the best briar pipe can subtly affect the taste of a fine smoking mixture. But not clay. Clay is a neutral material with no flavor of its own. Porous clay filters the tobacco naturally, absorbing juices and eliminating unpleasant odors other pipes often produce. Because it "breathes"—absorbing, then allowing condensed moisture to evaporate—a clay pipe smokes drier.

The first clay pipe smokers were probably Native Americans, who smoked them for both medicinal and ceremonial purposes. The "Marriage of Earth (clay) and Plant (tobacco) by Fire" was a cherished ritual. Sir Walter Raleigh introduced the American practice of pipe-smoking to the British Court in the sixteenth century, and the idea quickly spread throughout Europe. Men of all stations learned to enjoy the soul-satisfying pleasure of the clay pipe. Women, too, smoked clay pipes and were frequently offered a smoke during intermission at the theatre. The mistress of Louis XV, Madame de Pompadour, reportedly had a prized collection of more than 300 clay pipes.

Handmade from a unique mixture of four American clays and fired to a temperature of 2300° F., Lepeltier pipes produce an ideal marriage of strength and porosity, necessary for maintaining true tobacco taste.

Lepeltier pipes are available in plain or decorated versions. The beautifully detailed, full-color designs include a wildlife series; game birds; military, fraternal, and civic emblems; and an annual Christmas pipe.

Because of the asthetic appeal of the designs and craftsmanship, Lepeltier pipes are also collected by non-smokers.

Any pipe can be personalized. Most designs can be ordered with full bend, straight, or half-bend stems. Prices range from $15.00 to $35.00.

Wholesale available. All pipes are guaranteed. Ships UPS or U.S. mail. Payment by MasterCard, Visa, check, or money order.

Why the Lepeltier Clay Pipe provides such a wonderfully satisfying smoking experience

Porous double-walled bowl absorbs much of the smoke's tars and nicotines.

Imported ebonite stem.

Cork joint.

Hollow construction allows air to circulate and cool the smoke.

Flat base lets pipe stand upright, avoids messy spills.

High-fired glazed bowl with attractive decoration applied by hand.

The Lepeltier Clay Pipe offers you —

- All the true taste of your tobacco.
- Natural filtering of bitter tars and nicotine by porous clay bowl.
- Shatter resistance
- A pleasurably cool smoke. No "too hot to handle" bowl.

- Easy care. May be washed and rinsed occasionally under hot water, then air-dried overnight.
- Distinctive appearance that will attract admiring attention. Your pipe mellows and burnishes with use.

Maine Maid

25 Bow Street
Freeport, Maine 04032
(800) 232-MAINE

Maine Maid offers a selection of sweaters, hats, and mittens, and four styles of woolen capes. Starting with wool sheared from sheep raised in Maine, local Maine residents knit all the products in their own homes. The fabric for the capes is woven in a 107-year-old Maine mill, and the capes are sewn by Maine Maid's talented seamstresses.

The result is products that are as beautiful as they are practical. Maine Maid offers four cape designs: the *Romantic Hooded* is an mid-calf length cape with soft folds and a sumptuous hood. It is also available in a shorter length. Both styles are $130.00. The *Elegant Clasp* has a dramatic capelet to enhance this mid-calf length with a beautiful pewter clasp. It is $120.00. The *Comfortable Cowl* is $80.00. It falls slightly below

the knee, a fun, breezy cape with a roll collar. The *Casual Button* cape, versatile enough for jeans or a suit, has a warm wide wrap collar and corresponding cuffs. It is available for $100.00.

All capes are eighty percent wool and twenty percent nylon, and one size fits all. The colors available are wine, teal, royal, black, purple, red, and sage.

Maine Maid operates a retail shop at 25 Bow Street in Freeport, open daily from 10:00 A.M. to 5:00 P.M.

Free catalog. Wholesale available. No price quotes. Products guaranteed. Goods stocked and shipped UPS or U.S. Mail (on request only). Will ship to Canada. Orders shipped immediately upon receipt. Payment by MasterCard, Visa, check, or traveler's check.

Mayari Goatmilk Products

RR 1, Box 1560
Sedgwick, Maine 04676
(207) 359-2036

On a secluded spot on the Maine coast, the Donnell farm has its own dairy operation that utilizes state-tested milk from their goat herd. But they had an over-abundance of milk. Instead of wasting the nutrient-rich liquid, Mayra and Ariadne Donnell found a new way to pass the healthfulness of goat milk on to their customers.

Soap. The all-natural formula is a deep-cleansing product that is soothing to tender skin. The formula uses whole milk, honey as a skin toner, glycerine and vegetable oils for softening and moisturizing, and natural oils for a pleasing scent. The regular formula contains extra oil to help dry skin and is scented with a rose and hyacinth blend.

They also formulated a soap that contains oatmeal as its emollient, but without the roughness found in most other oatmeal-based soaps.

Their customers loved it. In addition to the soap, Mayari Goatmilk Products also makes Cuticle Cream, Lip Balm, Moisturizing Facial, and two Handwrought Wood Box gift packs.

A single bar of soap is $2.25. The Cuticle Cream is packed in a unique round wooden jar and sells for

$2.25. The Lip Balm is made from beeswax, safflower oil, and oil of rosemary and sells for $2.75.

The small Handwrought Wood Box gift pack contains two complexion bars of goatmilk soap and a jar of lip balm. The large Handwrought Wood Box gift pack contains two bath size bars of goatmilk soap. Gift pack items are surrounded with your choice of rose and hyacinth blend or patchouli potpourri.

Their retail store is at County Road, Box 1560, Sedgwick, Maine.

Free catalog. Wholesale available. No price quotes. Minimum order of three items. Goods are stocked; some made to order. Shipped within four weeks by UPS or U.S. mail. Product guaranteed. Payment by MasterCard, Visa, check, or money orders.

Mostrom and Chase Handweavers

36 Franklin Street
Newburyport, Massachusetts 01950
(508) 465-9586

The New England tradition of hard working, self-taught craftspeople continues in the work of Diane Mostrom-Chase and Fred Chase. When they began working at their looms in 1976, they started with a strong interest in historical textiles and early American folk patterns, and a desire to produce the finest handwoven cloth.

They wanted to create beautiful weavings that are "useful now and valued for many years." That phrase became their motto, and as their business grew and the number and kind of products they produce expanded, they have strived to maintain a quality and precision that is evident in each piece.

Mostrom and Chase specializes in weaving fine cotton table linen, table runners, and luxurious wool coverlets, blankets, and scarves. Each piece is individually handwoven in colonial New England patterns and designed for contemporary use, reflecting their interest in the preservation of the best Yankee traditions of fine artisanry.

Their hard work has paid off. Mostrom and Chase handwoven products are featured in many museum

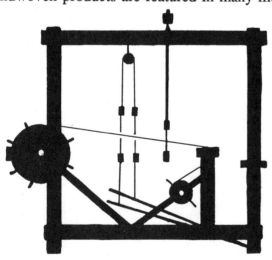

MOSTROM&CHASE

HANDWEAVERS

shops and have been authenticated by the Boston Museum of Fine Arts as traditional eighteenth century patterns. They also exhibit and sell to the Shakers in both Hancock Shaker Village and Canterbury, New Hampshire.

No where else is their reputation for fine work more evident than in their best-selling 100 percent wool Market Square coverlet. The Market Square design is a configuration in the traditional M's & O's pattern, suggesting the village square of a colonial marketplace. A shawl of their own design hugs your arms and shoulders. Their table linens are in various patterns and colors—the Lover's Knot, Leno Lace, Chariot Wheels, or Bronson Lace.

In 1990 Mostrom and Chase expanded their cotton line to include a wider selection of colors for border designs and colored cottons for their baby blankets, table scarves, and coverlets.

They also carry The Little Hand Weaver, a rigid heddle loom designed for weaving a variety of easy-to-make projects. A step-by-step introduction to the art of weaving, The Little Hand Weaver comes with everything you need to get started.

Placemats start at $7.50; napkins at $5.50; runners at $16.00. Table shawls are $44.00. Cotton Baby Blankets are $30.00. Bronson Lace Coverlet, Double, Queen, or King, $250.00.

Free catalog. Wholesale available. Ships UPS or U.S. mail within three weeks. Will ship to Canada. Payment by MasterCard, Visa, check, or money order.

North Country Textiles/Penobscot Weavers of Maine

Box 176, Route 175
South Penobscot, Maine 04476
(207) 326-4131

I n a renovated blueberry cannery overlooking Penobscot Bay, a small textile company has been working hard to build a reputation for excellence with fine, drapable fabric, meticulous tailoring, and concern for functional as well as beautiful designs.

Started in 1976 by Sheila Denny-Brown, Ron King, and Carole Ann Larson, North Country Textiles began by producing handwoven clothing. Word of their outstanding designs and the fine quality of their work spread, and as their business expanded, they added the Penobscot Weavers line, which covers their selection of throws, baby blankets, and fashion accessories.

They carry a wide variety of clothing, including capes, jackets, tops, scarves, shawls, and hats made in cotton, silk, and wool. Items for the home include blankets, towels, placemats, napkins, and pillows. The North Country Textile label still includes their custom handweaving business and the stock for their shop.

Every item from North Country Textiles is made completely in Maine using natural materials, most especially spun and dyed for them. A skilled weaver controls the production of each piece, which is carefully washed and steamed to preshrink and soften it, then labeled, tagged, and packaged.

Call them or write for a free catalog, or drop by their shop on Route 175 in South Penobscot. The store is open Monday through Saturday from 10:00 A.M. to 5:00 P.M. from Memorial Day to Columbus Day, but they welcome visitors year round—just call first so they can unlock the door for you.

Wholesale available. Goods are stocked and shipped UPS within three weeks. Will ship to Canada. Payment by American Express, MasterCard, Visa, check, or money order.

Brushed Mohair Throw   4' x 6' $130.00
   Available in Natural, Peach, Lavender, Blue,
      Grey Green, Cardinal, Teal
Wool Stripe Throw   4' x 6' $78.00
   Available in Naturals, Pink/Grey, Blues,
      Lavender/Green
Cotton Twill Throw   4' x 5' $50.00
   Available in Natural, Peach, Coral, Lavender,
      Periwinkle, Aqua

Baby Blanket   32" x 56" $48.00
   Available in Blue/Yellow, Lavender/Blue, Pink/
      Mint
Cotton Shawl   25" x 85" $70.00
   Available in Natural, Taupe, Grey
Silk/Wool Scarf   7.5" x 72" $32.00
   Available in Pink, Aqua, Brown, Blue/Green,
      Red/Purple, Indigo/Jade

Port Canvas

P. O. Box H-N
Kennebunkport, Maine 04046
(207) 985-9767

For more than 20 years, Port Canvas has had a tradition of quality that is obvious from the first glance at one of their bags: the thickness of the canvas, heavyweight zipper, and strong webbing. They use sailmaker's thread and double-stitch key seams. Their webbing extends all the way under the bags for extra strength.

Bags range from standard duffels, shaving kits, flight bags, and totes to bike and boot bags, log carriers, golf bags, and tool cases.

With thirteen canvas colors, three colors of trim, made-to-order monogramming and silkscreening, you can design a bag to your specifications, or order one they already have in stock. If you have a business, they can put your logo on a bag for either practical or promotional use. They have bags for fun, travel, and work. They'll even make a leash embroidered with your dog's name.

Port Canvas has a retail store on Ocean Avenue in Kennebunkport, open from 9:00 A.M. to 10:00 P.M. during the summer. Call (207) 967-2717 for off season hours.

Catalog available for $2.00. Wholesale available. Price quotes, for wholesalers only, by letter or phone. Products guaranteed. Shipped UPS unless otherwise requested. In stock items shipped within a few days. Made to order goods within two weeks. Rush service available. Will ship to Canada. Payment by American Express, MasterCard, Visa, check, or money order.

Sport Duffel	18" x 10"	$25.00
Cruiser Duffel	22" x 14"	35.00
Flight Bag	13" x 21" x 11"	74.00
Garment Travel Bag	46" x 24" x 5"	75.00
Eyeglass Case	7" x 3"	5.00
Port Canvas Brief	11" x 16" x 2.5"	40.00

PORT CANVAS

for the finest quality canvas goods

Shepherd's Flock

P. O. Box 131-NE
Townshend, Vermont 05353
(802) 365-4588

A quality product at a fair price, a belief in hard work, and the stubborn character needed to beat the odds against a small company is a typical Vermont attitude toward starting a new business. This is the foundation on which Shepherd's Flock was begun.

Kathy and Rick Hege started the company in 1978, and it remains a personal project for the two of them. "We are an extension of New England's past, a time when New England was the center of the leather trade with tanneries and shoe companies spread throughout, a gloving company in most every town. A time, long forgotten, when quality and craftsmanship were expected in all things."

The product line ranges from newly created stuffed toys to women's and men's jackets all made from shearling or slink lambskin. Slippers, with or without crepe soles, mittens, hats, anything you need to keep away the winter chill. And every product is created with the same attention because each is created by the same people.

For Kathy and Rick, everything is "made to order." Each piece is handcrafted after the order is received. They are always willing to handle "special needs" requests, and have been recognized for their efforts to provide products unavailable anywhere else, whether a single mitten for someone who has lost a hand, or special slippers for an elderly parent.

Kathy and Rick are superb craftspeople who are constantly striving to improve their work in order to better serve their customers.

The Shepherd's Flock retail store is on Route 30 in Townshend, open daily May through December from 10:00 A.M. to 5:00 P.M., closed only on Tuesday.

Prices range from $6.00 for a set of earmuffs to $400.00 for a man's three-quarter length coat. Any increase in prices generally take effect in August.

Free catalog. Products guaranteed within reason. Wholesale available. Products shipped by UPS or U.S. mail. Will ship (by mail) to Canada. Delivery within four weeks. Payment by MasterCard, Visa, check, or money order.

Slink Lambskin

Slink is baby lambskin, although no lamb is killed to obtain its skin. Farmers receive the greatest return on a full grown animal, and could never justify the loss of a lamb for just its skin. Slinks are from those lambs that have died of natural causes at about three weeks of age.

Most slink is from New Zealand, and is shipped to England for tanning, primarily for glove leather. Rick and Kathy import their slink from L.H. Nichols, Ltd. of England, the world's oldest and largest slink tanner. All slink leather from Nichols is top quality and completely hand-washable.

SHEPHERD'S ®
FLOCK

Stowe Woolens

RR #1, Box 1420
Stowe, Vermont 05672
(802) 253-9861
FAX (802) 253-8446

Deep in the heart of Vermont's Green Mountains, where travel is difficult when the winters are rough, a tradition of working at home has developed that has allowed many "cottage industries" to flourish even when the roads are impassable.

Stowe Woolens is a part of this New England tradition. Dedicated to offering their customers the finest wool sweaters, hats, and headbands, they know that by allowing home knitters to carefully handcraft each piece, they can guarantee a quality of work unsurpassed by any factory-constructed garment.

Stowe Woolens sweaters combine traditional handcrafted quality with a contemporary, fashionable look. Their designs reflect both a Scandinavian heritage and a sensitivity to the discriminating American market.

The wool for each sweaters is carefully selected. The skeins of wool are then dipped into dyes that are controlled so that they are color fast and resistant to fading. After the skeins are dried, they are shipped to Stowe and given to the home knitters to create the classic and unique designs of Stowe Woolens sweaters.

All the wool is 100 percent pure worsted, assuring comfort indoors and warmth outdoors. Their wide selection of designs and colors make choosing a sweater to match your individual style a pleasure.

Sweater prices start at $150.00; hats at $19.50; headbands at $17.00. Retail store on Main Street in Stowe.

Free catalog. Wholesale available. Goods stocked. Next day air available. Allow four to six week for custom knits. Shipped best way. Will ship to Canada. Payment by MasterCard, Visa, check, or money order.

Tapestries of New England

P. O. Box 396
St. Johnsbury, Vermont 05819
(802) 748-2829

Have you ever wanted your initials on a director's chair? How about a cloth handbag or travel bag that would really last?

Tapestries of New England offers beautifully textured embroidered canvas bags in a wide variety of colors that are handcrafted from the finest 18-ounce marine-weight cotton. Started in 1983 with a home-based company, Lorna Higgs' cottage industry now serves customers from across the United States who rely on Lorna's attentive service and individualized products. Among her 18 original designs are a cardinal, mallard duck, loon, cat, Scottish thistle, and iris. She works with each customer to design personalized embroidery for custom orders.

Tapestries of New England operates a retail store at 55 Eastern Avenue in St. Johnsbury, open Monday through Saturday from 9:00 A.M. to 5:00 P.M.

Free catalog. Price quotes available by letter or over the phone. Products shipped by UPS, unless otherwise requested, within three weeks.

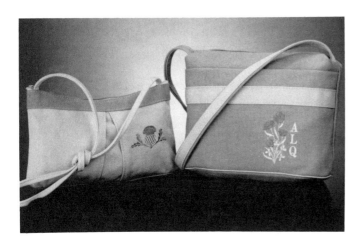

Sample List		
Handbag	11" x 9" x 4"	$38.50
Shoulder Bag	12" x 9" x 4"	36.50
Legal Briefcase	17.5 " x 11" x 4"	45.00
Oversized Tote	22" x 13" x 5"	42.00

TAPESTRIES OF NEW ENGLAND

Unique 1

P. O. Box 744
2 Bayview Street
Camden, Maine 04843
(207) 236-8717

Unique 1 is a sweater and yarn shop in the picturesque coastal village of Camden, Maine. The sweaters are made at home by dedicated knitters in the region using manual knitting looms. Each knitter completes an entire sweater from the knitting to the hand-crocheted seams and finishing touches, and signs her name to a tag. In the true Yankee tradition, each knitter has pride in her trade and respect for the quality of her work.

The wool sweaters are made of 100% natural oil wool from Maine sheep. A special technique used in processing the wool preserves the natural lanolin and other oils that provide extra warmth and water resistence. These sweaters will actually shed water and keep you warm if they get wet. They are available in natural sheep color or dyed in fifteen subtle shades like blueberry, mountain cranberry, mallard green, goldenrod, wood violet, or dusty rose.

The cotton sweaters are made of 100 percent combed cotton yarn cultivated and harvested in the San Joaquin Valley in California. The cotton yarn is carefully combed to remove the short fibers, then lightly twisted and kettle dyed. The cotton sweaters have been preshrunk to assure proper sizing. They are available in more than 20 fashion colors like periwinkle blue, French red, city nights navy, mauve, or porcelain pink.

Unique 1 sweaters are available in a variety of styles that range from basics to the whimsical. They also offer jackets, hats, socks, and the original, Maine made Baby Bag. Also available are skein yarns and hand knitting supplies as well as cone yarns and machine knitting supplies.

Retail store open daily from 9:00 A.M. to 5:00 P.M. during the winter; 9:00 A.M. to 9:00 P.M. during the summer. Wholesale available. All products are guaranteed. Catalog is available for $2.00. Ships UPS to the United States and Canada within three weeks. Payment by American Express, MasterCard, Visa, check, or money order.

The Boater
A wonderful oversized wool sweater
$58.00

Wool Hats
Moose, sheep, or loon designs
$28.00

Classic Reindeer Wool Sweater
Everyone should have a reindeer sweater
at least once.
$62.00

Cotton Whale Sweater
Cotton Boxy Style Crew Neck
$68.00

Cotton Sailboat Sweater
A crewneck with a double thick mock rib at hem,
cuff, and neck that keeps its shape
$68.00

Cotton V-pullover
A wonderful appealing look
$55.00

Western Maine Weavers

13 Pearl Street
Camden Maine 04843
(207) 236-4069

N ancy Lubin takes the ancient art of fine quality handweaving, and gives it a unique twist. Since 1976 Nancy has used her talent as a designer to create individualized, one-of-a-kind throws, scarves, and stoles for her clients.

She starts with a photograph or two, and swatches of fabric, wallpaper, carpet, or paint. Then, after a telephone conversation with the customer to gather even more information, Nancy carefully designs a pattern and chooses the colors. Her painstaking selection process assures that only the very best yarns are used. These are individually handwoven into the finished product, assuring straight, finished edges that are complemented with handknotted fringes.

Photo by Lynn Karlin

Western Maine Weavers

Much as a classical artist works with a carefully chosen canvas, it is with these fine yarns that Nancy Lubin works her own artistry in design and color. The result may be subtle, heather-shaded tones in an exquisite stole, or vibrant splashes of color in a stunning scarf, but it always identifies her unique style.

Nancy has created throws that have appeared in major home design magazines. She also exhibits her works at prestigious national craft fairs and national trade shows.

In addition to her personalized designs, she also maintains an extensive stock of finished throws, stoles, and scarves designed from an exhaustive palette of 110 colors, including contemporary fashion colors as well as "forecast" colors.

Standard sizes for the throws start at 42" x 54" for the gift size and include a 48" x 72" throw for a regular size bed. Larger sizes can be made on request. The gift size throws start at $145.00, and throws for regular beds range from $225.00 to $375.00.

Nancy handles retail sales at 13 Pearl Street in Camden.

Wholesale available. Price quotes by letter or phone. Products guaranteed. Shipped by UPS unless otherwise requested. Will ship to Canada. Shipping time varies. Payment by MasterCard, Visa, check, or money order.

FOR KIDS OF ALL AGES

HOBBIES, CRAFTS, AND TOYS

1840 House/Jacqueline Designs

237 Pine Point Road
Scarborough, Maine 04074
(207) 883-5403

I n 1970, a friend persuaded Jacqueline Hansen to enroll in a rug hooking class at Berry's of Maine, a rug hooking and needlecraft supply shop. Jacqueline enjoyed the class, never thinking that it would lead her to buy Berry's of Maine and combine it with her already established interior decorating shop, The Georgian House.

Jacqueline went on to teach rug hooking at the YWCA in Portland, and between her business and her teaching, she began to receive requests for special patterns and designs. As a result, in 1982, she began publishing her designs in her 1840 House catalog and selling the patterns by mail order.

Jacqueline designs in a variety of modern and traditional styles, and offers more than 300 patterns in such categories as rosemaling, crewel, fruits, flowers, oriental designs, stained glass, and primitives.

She also stocks a complete supply list: custom designing wools, frames, cutters—everything the rug hooker could need. Custom designs and color planning are available to the customer who wishes to work more closely with Jacqueline.

Prices for the hooking patterns range from $3.50 to $35.00. Prices for the hooking kits range from $18.00 to $150.00.

Retail store at 237 Pine Point Road in Scarborough. Call for hours.

Catalog available for $5.50. Wholesale available. Price quotes for custom orders only. Products guaranteed. Goods in stock shipped within one week. Custom orders may take up to four weeks. Ships UPS or U.S. mail. Will ship to Canada. Payment by check or money order.

The Anchorage, Inc./Dyer Boats

57 Miller Street
Warren, Rhode Island 02885-0403
(401) 245-3300

During World War II, the U.S. Navy asked The Anchorage to design a boat that could act as a lifeboat for nine people on mine sweepers, for aircraft rescue, and on PT boats. That was asking too much from a conventional dinghy design, so they modified it, creating the Dyer Dhow hull, a dinghy so different in design that they were able to patent it, and have been producing it ever since.

Every Dyer boat is handcrafted so each one is slightly different, but they all have an unmatched quality, style, and superior durability from the 7' 9" "Midget" to the 12.5' Dyer Dhow.

The first Dyer Dinghies were made of wood, but today the craftspeople at The Anchorage use hand lay-up fiberglass for a boat that is both strong and light. Mahogany or teak is used for the seats and transom reinforcement, and all hardware is solid bronze and stainless steel.

In sailing models, the centerboard trunk is molded integrally with the hull. The unsinkable Sitka spruce spars are hand turned, and will not sink if dropped overboard. Options, like custom hull colors and molded-in personal identification lettering, let you personalize each boat.

The base prices for the dinghies start at $1435.00 for the rowing model of the 7'11" Midget. The sailing model of the Midget is $2280.00. The 9' Dhow® is $1470.00 (rowing) and $2320 (sailing), and the 10' D Dink is $2095 (rowing) and $3625 (sailing). The largest dinghy—the 12.5' Dhow®—is available only in the sailing model and lists for $4980.

Call or write for more information. Ships nationwide and to Canada, F.O.B. Warren, Rhode Island.

BlueJacket Shipcrafters, Inc.

School Street
P. O. Box 425
Stockton Springs, Maine 04981
(802) 448-5567

BlueJacket is America's premier model ship kit maker. Their strict adherence to detail and authenticity in their historical models requires years of research before a final kit is prepared.

Their "flagship" model is the USS Constitution, portrayed as she was during her heyday, 1812-1815. The author of the plans and instructions, Laurence Arnot, spent several years going through the archives at the Constitution Museum. He read repair logs, took numerous measurements aboard the ship, researched vendor's invoices dating back to 1800, and spent hours with the ship's logs. The step-by-step instruction book has more than 100 line drawings and photographs and the kit includes 2,600 fittings of brass and britannia pewter, and 20 different sizes of rigging cords.

It sounds like a massive job, but it is the same amount of detail and attention that BlueJacket has given all of their models, from the tall ships to the Civil War ironclads to the World War II destroyers. They have both pre-carved hull kits and plank-on-frame kits. They are also a leading custom caster of britannia metal, and offer one of the country's largest selections of specialized fittings. Books and tools for the serious modeler complete their catalog.

You, too, can have that old-fashioned feeling of accomplishment, plus the pleasure of having created a thing of beauty and lasting value. Each inch of the vessel will be your own creation—and your own reward.

The plank-on-frame kit for the *America* is $235.00, and the pre-carved hull kit for the *Constitution* is $350.00. Other kits range from $75.00 to $300.00.

The BlueJacket Shipcrafters retail outlet is in Stockton Springs, and is open Monday through Friday from 9:00 A.M. to 5:00 P.M.

Catalog available for $2.00, refundable with purchase. Wholesale available. Price quotes by phone or letter. Minimum order of $20.00 (for charge orders). Products stocked, guaranteed, and shipped within one week by UPS. Will ship to Canada. Payment by MasterCard or Visa.

Bowers and Merena Galleries, Inc.

P. O. Box 1224
Wolfeboro, New Hampshire 03894
603-569-5095

Bowers and Merena holds a unique place in the world of collectible coins. Since 1953, they have been the leading suppliers of rare coins to collectors, museums, dealers, and investors. Located deep in the heart of New England, Bowers and Merena have access to old-time estates, collections, and other properties.

They also publish *Rare Coin Review,* which lists thousands of available coins, from silver dollars and gold coins to commemoratives and colonial coins, such as Pine Tree shillings and other New England issues.

The magazine also features informational and research features, book reviews, stories of sales and auctions, and market reports. It is a fascinating and comprehensive view of the world of the numismatist, whether you're interested in a $6.00 dime or the 1793 American one-cent piece worth $97,500.

Coins are sold worldwide by mail. Each piece comes with a 30-day guarantee of satisfaction, and an unlimited guarantee of authenticity.

Bowers and Merena is also a leading publisher of reference books and manuals pertaining to rare coins.

A copy of *Rare Coin Review* is available for $5.00. Most coins and other products are in stock, and will be shipped by U.S. mail within one week. Payment by American Express, MasterCard, Visa, check, or money order.

CedarWorks, Inc.

Route 1, Box 640-NEM
Rockport, Maine 04856
(800) 233-7757 (outside Maine)
(800) 244-7757 (inside Maine)
(207) 236-3183

Duncan and Susan Brown, the owners of Cedar-Works, honor the Indians of Maine for their deep love and respect for nature, and are inspired by the Indians' sense of responsibility for taking care of the earth. The Browns are also seriously concerned with the health and safety of children.

The combination of these two interests led Susan and Duncan to create playsets that are safe for both the children and the environment. The Browns know that other parents share their concerns because of the demand for wood playsets that do not need to be pressure-treated with chemicals.

CedarWorks Playsets are made with 4"x4" splinter-free cedar and shock-resistant ash ladder rungs. Cedar resists rotting naturally and effectively. In fact, Cedar-Works guarantees the cedar in their playsets to last for at least twenty years.

Each set is free-standing and easy to assemble. There's no digging or cement with any of the ten basic playsets, whether it's the compact MicMac Twin Teepee or the mammoth Samoset Twin Jungle. An exciting variety of optional accessories include slides, rope ladders, sandboxes, swings, canvas tenting, fort fences, and more. A playful spirit is included free.

The Builders Association of Greater Boston presented this unique Maine company with the coveted *Judge's Choice* Award at the New England Home Show. The judges acknowledged CedarWorks for its treatment of people as well as for its child-safe philosophy and the superior quality of its playsets.

One other way the Browns have honored the Indians of Maine is that most of their playsets have names taken from the Indians' languages. And if you don't speak Abnaki, Micmac, or Maliseet, they include a pronunciation guide.

Prices for the playsets range from $750.00 to $1,675.00.

CedarWorks has a retail store on Route One in Rockport. They are open Monday through Friday from 8:30 A.M. to 4:30 P.M. and Saturdays in season from 9:00 A.M. to 4:30 P.M.

Free catalog. Price quotes by letter or phone. Playsets and accessories guaranteed. Goods stocked and shipped within two weeks by truck. Some items can be shipped UPS. Payment by MasterCard, Visa, check, or money order.

Connecticut Cane and Reed

P. O. Box 762
Manchester, Connecticut 06040
(800) 227-8498 (outside Connecticut)
(203) 646-6586

The art of weaving cane and reeds into beautiful baskets and furniture is a craft that is several centuries old, yet it is an art that is still growing and being practiced by skilled craftspeople. A pattern or basket style is adapted by a basketmaker, picked up by others, and before long a distinctive new style is a recognized part of the field. There are, for instance, Nantucket and Shaker baskets, push-bottom and indented-style baskets, fine radio, Swedish, or herringbone weaves.

The Connecticut Cane and Reed Company specializes in all of these and more. They supply anyone who is interested in basketweaving or caning with all the materials needed. If you are a novice, they have kits to get you started and more than 150 books of patterns, instructions, and history. For the more experienced caner, they have a wide selection of materials, including pre-woven cane for immediate use or repair.

Their selection of materials includes natural chair cane, cane webbing, binding cane, reed spline, fiber rush, oak splint, flat reed, flat oval reed, round reed, ash splint, seagrass, and slab rattan. Prices of the pre-

woven webbing start at $3.55 for a 12-foot wide natural cane piece. Basket weaving kits start at $9.95. Furniture frames start at $7.95 for a small ash footstool.

Connecticut Cane and Reed Company also carries tools, basket molds, Shaker tape, and furniture frames. They have an experienced staff trained to answer questions and recommend the proper materials. They'll help you chose whatever you need to be a part of one of the oldest crafts in the world.

Catalog available for $1.00. Wholesale available. Product guaranteed. Goods are stocked and shipped UPS or U.S. mail the same day the order is received. Will ship to Canada. Payment by American Express, MasterCard, Visa, check or money order.

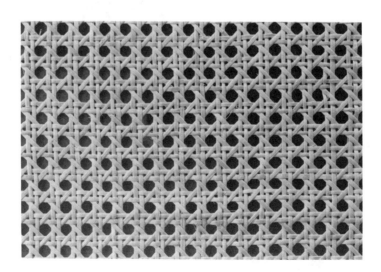

Elwood Turner

Box HC 132
Morrisville, Vermont 05661
(802) 888-3375

When Ed Loewenton founded the Elwood Turner Company in 1978, he had a simple plan in mind. "A toy should demand something of us; it should be good for something more than just passing a little time." And over the next twelve years, the company has been built by standing by its motto: "To Challenge, To Educate, To Entertain."

The Elwood Turner Company makes toys and games, some traditional, some they design. They are made of wood: simple, sturdy, and handsome. And *everybody* who works there is a quality control inspector.

Their games—Jumpo® and Ntangle™—are difficult enough for teenagers and adults. They are games of intellect, not chance. The Easy Winner™ Top and Busy Wheel™ challenge the coordination, patience, and determination of youngsters six years and up.

But the centerpiece of the Elwood Turner line is My Very Own Rattle®, an elegant update of a traditional woodturner's exercise. It is simple yet superior to all other rattles and teething toys. It's safe, beautiful, durable, and well crafted. My Very Own Rattle® is heavy enough to challenge a five-month-old, and its moving rings and complex textures encourage tactile learning.

All of the toys and games from Elwood Turner are made with an uncomprising quality. Jumpo® retails for $6.50; Ntangle™ is $12.00. The Busy Wheel™ is $6.80, the Easy Winner™ Top is $5.00, and My Very Own Rattle® is $14.95.

But everything is not just for kids. They also make solid rock maple rolling pins for pies and pasta, and decorative candleholders with fireproof metal cups.

So who *is* Elwood Turner? He is an old-fashioned, hard-working fellow who likes kids, and believes in a future worth working toward, and past worth preserving. He no longer works with the company—he's very old—but he visits late at night to inspect what they do, making sure that their work meets his high standards. He says he's a great-great-great-grand-nephew of Davy Crockett. But he could be a distant cousin of Santa Claus on his mother's side. They're not sure.

Free catalog. Wholesale available. No price quotes. Products guaranteed. Goods stocked and shipped UPS or U.S. Mail within six weeks, although shipping time is usually less than one week. Will ship to Canada. Retail orders prepaid only, by check or money order.

The Enchanted Doll House

Dept. NBM
P. O. Box 1616 (mail orders only)
Manchester, Connecticut 06040
(800) 243-9110 (outside Connecticut)
(203) 646-5008 (inside Connecticut and Customer Service)

The Enchanted Doll House is a special place. Nestled among Vermont's Green Mountains is an 1850s farmhouse, now a 12-room shop, crammed full of dolls, miniatures, toys for all ages, stuffed animals, marionettes, gift accessories, dollhouse kits, decorating materials, and much more.

The doll collection is extensive and always in the process of being expanded, from dolls made of vinyl, cloth, bisque, felt, and wood to reproductions of famous antique dolls and newly designed dolls from some of today's most talented designers. Robin Woods created Victories Ann, a contemporary version of an antique French doll, just for The Enchanted Doll House. A Snow White and the Seven Dwarfs set was created by R. John Wright Dolls in collaboration with Margaret Armstrong Hand, whose husband was the director of the original Snow White movie. Other dolls, from Madame Alexander's Party Girls to the Steiff bears will delight children of any age.

But dolls are only the beginning. There is also a myriad of toys for infants and toddlers—from soft cuddly crib toys to wooden toy trains and cars—and an extensive list of children's books. The miniature collection is exceptional, with many items especially handcrafted by local artisans just for The Enchanted Doll House.

The price range for the dolls starts at less than $20.00 for such items as the exquisite prima Mousarina and extends to more than $300.00 for some of the collectible dolls. Other toy groups have similar price ranges.

The catalog describes each item in careful detail with personal comments about each item, bits of history about a product or the shop, and full-color photos.

The retail shop for The Enchanted Doll House is on Route 7, 2½ miles north of Manchester Center, Vermont. It is open Monday through Saturday from 9:00 A.M. to 5:30 P.M. and on Sundays from 10:00 A.M. to 5:30 P.M. Call (802) 362-1327 for more information.

Catalog available for $3.00. No wholesale. Price quotes by letter or phone. Goods stocked with some made to order. Products guaranteed and shipped within three weeks by UPS, U.S. mail, or customer's preference. Will ship to Canada. Payment by American Express, MasterCard, Visa, Discover, check, or money order.

Halcyon Yarn

12 School Street
Bath, Maine 04530
(800) 341-0282 (outside Maine)
(800) 349-7909 (inside Maine)

In 1972 Halcyon Schomp opened a tiny hand-weaving supply store. It was a simple start, but by working closely with her customers and teaching weaving at night, her business boomed. In just a few years it was the finest shop of its kind, and in 1979, Halcyon expanded into mail order with the most comprehensive yarn sample set ever produced, her original Yarn Store in a Box®.

"What you have in mind, we put in your hand."

From its turn-of-the-century warehouse in Bath, Halcyon provides weavers and knitters a wider selection of supplies than any other single source. They feature looms, books, how-to video tapes, computer software, basketry material, sweater kits, accessory equipment, and—the cornerstone of their business—yarn: three styles of rug wools in more than 100 shades, Victorian mohairs, Gemstone silks, Scottish worsted, Newport linen, and their own hand-dyed Halcyon Yarn. All of these help them live up to their motto: "What you have in mind, we put in your hand."

The spectacular variety of products offered allows you to spend time creatively at your craft instead of searching for materials.

Halcyon Yarn operates a retail shop in Bath. Call for hours.

Free catalog. The Yarn Store in a Box® sample kit is $33.00, $10 of which is refundable with a $50 purchase. Price quotes by letter or phone. Products guaranteed. Goods stocked and shipped by UPS or U.S. mail within two weeks. Will ship to Canada. Payment by personal check only.

Yarn			Equipment	
Halcyon Rug Wool	4-ounce skein	$17.00/pound	36" Heavy Duty Raddle	$18.50
Nehalem	2-ounce tube	3.35/tube	15" Boat shuttle	19.00
Harrisville Shetland	3.5-ounce skein	5.70/skein	AVL Handshuttle	36.00
Scottish Tapestry Wool	4-ounce skein	6.10/skein	Niddy-noddy	17.50
3/2 Pearl Cotton	180 yard cone	3.30/cone	Louet Assembled Drum Carder	225.00
2/20s Pearl Silk	315-yard mini-cone	5.35/cone	Schacht Spinning Wheel	350.00
Surrey Tweed	425-yard mini-cone	5.50/cone	McMorran Yarn Balance	16.00
Candlelight Tussah	3-ounce skein	48.00/pound	Harrisville 22" 4 Harness Kit	320.00
Taffy	8.8-ounce cone	19.00/pound	Round Reed (1.75mm) 900-foot roll	7.30/roll
2/24 Merino Wool	800-yard cone	4.40/cone	Flat Reed (.25in) 350-foot roll	7.30/roll

Handmade By Peg® Porcelain Dolls

P. O. Box 514 RH
Gales Ferry, Connecticut 06335
(203) 464-8348

If you enjoy dolls—as a hobby, an investment, or as keepsakes—write for Peg Donahue's catalog. Every one of her dolls is carefully handmade and lovingly dressed in handmade clothes (even undergarments). Peg uses only the finest lace, fabrics and ribbons. Ribbon color choices for baby dolls are white, pink, blue, rose, lavender, or off-white.

Most of Peg's dolls are reproductions of antiques, although she also has a few that are made from original molds. Her dolls include French and German heirloom reproductions, and even Kewpie dolls. Among Peg's German dolls, for instance, are Mein Liebling, a lovely serene-looking doll that is all porcelain with a jointed body, and Bruno Schmidt, another all porcelain doll with long blond hair and an outfit covered with tiny flowers.

Peg's French dolls include Celeste, a reproduction of a Steiner original, which has a porcelain head with glass eyes and a French jointed composition body.

Laughing Jumeau has a porcelain head and beautiful molded teeth. Her body is jointed porcelain and she has long curls that complement her brick rose print dress.

All dolls are available in either light or dark flesh colors.

Peg also stocks doll kits. Prices for the doll kits range from $6.00 for a six-inch Baby Aron to $65.00 for a 17.5-inch Byelo.

Catalog available for $2.00. Wholesale available. Price quotes by letter or phone. Products guaranteed. Some goods are stocked; most are made to order and shipped within four to six weeks. Ships UPS or U.S. mail. Will ship to Canada. Payment by MasterCard, Visa, check, or money order.

Averill Baby (pictured here)	$235.00
Mein Liebling	160.00
Kewpie Doll	38.00
Bruno Schmidt	235.00
Celeste	395.00
Laughing Jumeau	210.00

HANDMADE BY PEG®
Porcelain Dolls

Hearthside Quilts

Box 429
Shelburne, Vermont 05482
(800) 451-3533

If you have ever wanted to try quilting but were unsure how to start, give Hearthside a call. They have quilt kits in a wide selection of patterns, styles, and difficulty levels.

If you are a novice, try a quilt from the Level One selections. Straight seams make them easy to sew, but there's nothing simple about the beauty of a traditional "Log Cabin" pattern, a "Double Irish Cross," or a "Three Rail Fence" placemat.

The Level Two patterns include the "Eight Point Star" and "The Kaleidoscope." Level Three features patterns such as the "Double Wedding Ring," the "Dresden Plate," and "The Pinwheel," while Level Four includes some of the prettiest quilts, such as the "Daisy Chain" appliqué quilt, the "Dutch Tulip," and "The Primrose."

Each kit comes with precision pre-cut pieces for the top, thread, instructions, a quilting needle, batting, and backing. The standard kit includes 100% polyester batting, and a 100% cotton muslin backing. They also have 100% wool batting available for an heirloom quality.

Hearthside Quilts can also supply frames, forms, thimbles, thread, needles, hoops, and many more items for the home quilter.

In addition to their piece and appliqué quilts, Hearthside offers kits for pillows and placemats, and, on request, larger sizes and pre-sewn quilts. Pre-sewn quilts can be sent in one of three stages: with the top pieced, with the completed top tied to the batting and backing for you to quilt, and completely sewn and quilted. Pre-sewn quilts are completed by machine.

Carpenter's Square Design

Hearthside also offers designs from the Shelburne Museum collection of more than 900 designs.

Prices for the pre-cut kits range from $37.50 for the twin sizes to $169.50 for king sizes. Extra yardage can be ordered. Prices vary with the difficulty of the pattern.

Sewn quilt prices range from $55.00 for a sewn top in a simpler pattern to $425.00 for a machine quilted king size appliqué pattern.

Free catalog. Products shipped UPS. Orders outside the continental U.S. shipped by parcel post. Will ship to Canada. Payment by American Express, Master-Card, Visa, Discover, check or money order.

The Laughing Whale

174 Front Street
Bath, Maine 04530
(207) 443-5732

On May 3, 1851, a schooner yacht was launched and sailed for England within a month. Participating in a race sponsored by the Royal Yacht Club, she won by a wide margin, thus becoming one of the most famous yachts in history. The race, now called the America's Cup, was even named for her. Now you can own a high quality wooden model of that famous yacht.

The Laughing Whale manufactures and sells high quality wooden model kits of both historic and everyday ships and boats, from a simple dory to a complex replica of the three-masted *Joseph Conrad*. Each boat is a true scale model, and builders can choose from display models or those suitable for remote control.

Each kit comes with blueprints, instructions, sailcloth metal fittings, rigging cord, and wooden parts. The catalog features a short history of most of the boats.

The Laughing Whale operates a retail shop at 174 Front Street in Bath. During the summer it is open Monday through Saturday from 10:00 A.M. to 5:00 P.M. Winter hours are from 10:00 A.M. to 3:30 P.M.; closed Wednesday.

Catalog available for $1.00. Kits range in price from $18.95 to $165.95. Wholesale available to hobby shops, etc. Products guaranteed. Goods stocked and shipped within three weeks by UPS. Ten percent shipping charge applied. Payment by American Express, MasterCard, Visa, Discover, check, or money order.

The Friendship Sloop

Joseph Conrad

Learning Materials Workshop

274 North Winooski Avenue
Box R
Burlington, Vermont 05401
(802) 862-8399

As a young girl, Karen Hewitt often visited a friend in New York City who had lots of toys and some window planters full of dirt and pebbles. The piles of toys would lie ignored as Karen and her friend played for hours with the dirt and pebbles.

Today, Karen Hewitt runs a company that makes what she calls "the next best thing to dirt and stones." Her Learning Materials Workshop creates and produces high-quality design and construction toys for young children and playful adults.

Child development experts call these toys "open-ended." Open-ended toys are meant to spark a child's imagination and creativity by having more than just one use and more than one way to use them.

The Learning Materials Workshop's series of cubes, bobbins, beams, frame sections, dowels, arches, and prisms are designed to engage children in active and creative play. The pieces from different sets all interconnect, allowing the size and challenge of a set to grow as the child does.

Each toy is carefully crafted in Vermont from maple and birch hardwoods and finished with non-toxic paints. There are also special toys even grown-ups will want to play with, such as Prismatics and Spectra.

Constructed to last a lifetime, Learning Material Workshop toy sets have four times won the prestigious Parent's Choice Award, given to toys that "...best exemplify our criteria of purposefulness, child involvement, aesthetic appeal, safety, and, of course, playfulness and fun."

The time Karen spent playing in the dirt has finally paid off.

The Cubes, Bobbins, Beams set is $48.00. Thingamabobin is $35.00. Prismatics is $185.00, and Spectra is $75.00.

Catalog available for $1.00, refundable with purchase. Wholesale available. Products guaranteed. Goods are stocked and shipped by UPS or U.S. mail within three to four weeks. Will ship to Canada. Payment by MasterCard, check, or money order.

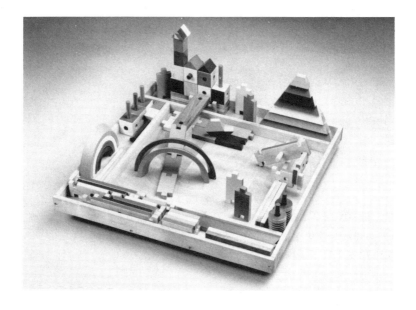

Lucretia's Pieces

R. F. D. #1, Box 501
Windsor, Vermont 05089
(802) 436-3006

There's a woman in Windsor, Vermont, who intentionally tries to irritate people. She makes her living trifling with people's good natures—and they love it. Lucretia's Pieces custom makes wooden jigsaw puzzles that are individualized for each buyer. Each puzzle is cut by hand with such precision that a

completed puzzle can be lifted its edges and not fall apart.

The picture can be anything you want—from classic fine art to a photo of your Uncle Fred. Lucretia also has hundreds of prints available as some people want Lucretia to surprise them because they don't want to see what the puzzle looks like ahead of time. (The boxes do not include a picture of the completed puzzle.)

But don't be lulled by the beauty of these puzzles. They are cunning, devious, and filled with tricks that make die-hard puzzlers squirm and fume (with affection). They may have irregularly shaped edges, open

spaces or dozens of other traps to throw you off. They are delightful, infectious fun!

Best of all, each puzzle is filled with silhouettes, shapes, words, and surprises that can be personalized for the recipient. If you have a favorite pet, a 1942 Pontiac, or the secret nickname of "Snookums," watch out, because it will quite likely show up as a piece of your puzzle. That's why these puzzles make unforgettable personal gifts.

Catalog available for $1.00. Prices start at around $200.00. Since each one is custom-made, call or write for a price quotation. Products guaranteed. Shipped by U.S. mail, unless otherwise requested, within six weeks, possibly longer at Christmas. Payment by MasterCard, Visa, check, or money order.

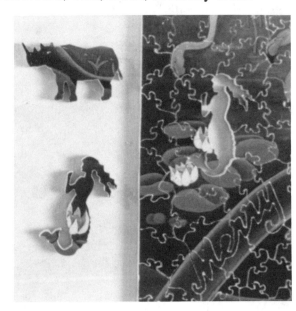

Macomber Looms

P. O. Box 186
Beech Ridge Road
York, Maine 03909
(207) 363-2808

Making handwoven fabric is a respected and traditional craft that allows each weaver to express design and artistic creativity. It is an art form as distinctive as painting or sculpting. Yet just as a painter must have the right brushes and colors and the sculptor the right chisels, the weaver must have a good reliable loom to bring the artwork alive.

Since 1936 Macomber Looms has been building high-quality and durable looms. Leroy W. Macomber revolutionized the hand loom in 1936 with his introduction of the AD-A-HARNESS Loom: a loom that was expandable enough that a weaver could add harnesses up to the capacity of the frame, and flexible enough that the loom could continue to grow with the weaver's interest, ability, and financial resources.

Today, Macomber Looms is a family-owned business that is still dedicated to preserving a tradition of craftsmanship and innovation by manufacturing only those products which meet the quality standards set in 1936. Over the past ten years, Macomber has been a leader in computerizing the handweaving process so that they are now able to offer both traditional as well as technically advanced looms.

Their catalog features the textile design and handweaving tools that they have developed through careful research and testing. Each one represents their philosophy that neither economy and quality nor flexibility and effectiveness are mutually exclusive, but are all elements of a sound design.

Yet, first and foremost, a loom must be a good reliable tool. Macomber uses only the strongest, most durable materials available. From their small portable Baby Macs™ to their large folding looms and on to their uniquely designed tools, Macomber provides the weaver with effective, reliable tools.

Prices for the looms range from $435.00 for a small four harness 16-inch Baby Mac™ to $8400.00 for a folding Extra Large Mac™.

Free catalog. Products guaranteed. Price quotes by letter or phone. Looms shipped by common carrier. Smaller parts sent by UPS or parcel post. Some goods stocked. Most looms are made to order. Orders shipped within ten weeks. Will ship to Canada. Payment by MasterCard, Visa, check, or money order.

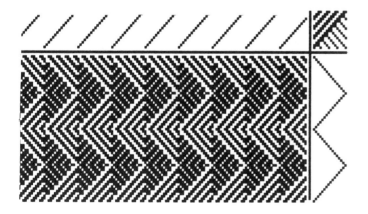

Mad River Canoe

P. O. Box 610
Mad River Green
Waitsfield Vermont 05673
(802) 496-3127

An old Native American legend tells the story of the Confident Rabbit who sits amid the ferns, pipe in hand, fearless even of the lynx, his mortal enemy, who is never far away. The rabbit is confident of his own ability to succeed; he trusts his own strength and cleverness.

The seal of the Confident Rabbit is the guarantee from the craftspeople at Mad River Canoe that they have done the best possible job in creating your canoe.

Every Mad River Canoe is handmade, built with the skill of a master craftsperson. Hundreds of hours of research are invested in finding the best materials and the most efficient design. Thus, aerospace technology and hand- made craftsmanship meet in a combination that clearly represents the best of both worlds.

Because the craftspeople at Mad River also use the canoes they build, they know that a canoe can reflect your personal style and have developed a series of options to customize your canoe. Choose a favorite color, add a sail or a drop-in rowing rig, a caned seat back or an anchor outrigger. They also offer a full line of paddles and personal gear.

The canoes with fiberglass, kevlar, Royalex, and hybrid constructions. The catalog details the differences in hull designs, and each canoe has a listing for keel line configuration, hull shape, and symmetry. Mad River will make recommendations as to which canoe would best fit what activity. This makes it easy for even a novice to choose and outfit a canoe.

Because each canoe is handmade, they are more expensive than some factory-made boats. A Royalex Plus "Flashback II" (13') starts at $729.00, and the prices run up to $3,799.00 for a Hybrid "Grand Laker" (21'). Mad River Canoe does offer a finance plan that can be arranged through any of Mad River's authorized dealers.

The Mad River retail store is in the Mad River Shopping Green in Waitsfield, and is open Monday through Friday from 9:00 A.M. to 5:00 P.M.

Free catalog, price list, and list of dealers. Wholesale available. Price quotes by letter or telephone. Canoes and gunwales ordered by mail are shipped by common carrier in the U.S. Other equipment shipped by UPS, U.S. mail, or Federal Express. Goods are stocked and shipped within one week. Payments by MasterCard, Visa, check, or money order.

Kevin Martin, Boatbuilder

RFD #1, Box 441
Epping, New Hampshire 03042
(603) 679-5153

At the turn of the century, J. Henry Rushton and W. P. Stephens were among several boatbuilders whose innovative designs and high quality craftsmanship were unmatched. They made lightweight, clinker-built canoes for use in the lakes and rivers of the northeast, and decked sailing canoes for traveling long distances.

They used the lapstrake method of construction, which yielded canoes that are very light. The combination of the closely spaced hardwood ribs plus the double thickness of the planking at the laps made them more durable than most people suspected.

Today, Kevin Martin carries on the tradition of the lapstrake canoe. "I build my canoes using the same methods as the builders in Rushton's time, starting with a keel of white or red oak that is rabbeted to receive the gardboard planks. The stems are of the roots of hackmatack trees which are light but durable and the grain follows the curve of the stem.

"The planking is quarter-inch white cedar with each strake lapping over the one below it and fastened to each other with copper clinch tacks."

Kevin builds several open canoes from the 10'6" Wee Lassie ($1,800) to the 17' Canadian Ugo Model ($2,500) made with family trips in mind.

Kevin's sailing canoes are decked boats constructed with the lapstrake method following the plans of W. P. Stephens. "For many years, these decked sailing canoes were thought of as the 'perfect canoe,' meaning they provided for all the canoe traveler's needs. They paddled well, sailed well, provided room to sleep in, cook in, and in foul weather a tent could be set up over the cockpit."

His sailing canoes include the 14'3" Princess model ($4,500) and the 12' Rob Roy ($3,500).

Kevin also builds the traditional Adirondack Guideboat ($3,500 to $4,500), and offers a selection of canoe accessories such as paddles and folding seats.

Catalog available for $2.00. All boats are guaranteed; Kevin will repair any canoe damaged in normal use. Price quotes by letter or mail. All boats made to order; allow three to six months for construction. Boats shipped by common carrier unless customers wish to pick them up. Will ship to Canada. Payment by check only.

Martin Marine

Box 251—Goodwin Road
Kittery Point, Maine 03905
(207) 439-1507

In 1971, Arthur Martin revolutionized recreational rowing by introducing a new design for a racing shell. For years, Martin, a naval architect who had spent World War II designing warships, had been experimenting with new designs for a fiberglass kayak. He lengthened the standard thirteen- to fifteen-foot design to sixteen feet, and fitted the hull with a sliding seat to make the rowing easier. The combination of the speed and rowing ease of a racing shell with the stability and strength of a kayak resulted in a craft that even a novice could learn to handle within minutes.

Martin called his new craft the Alden Ocean Shell, named for the celebrated yacht designer John Alden, and opened Martin Marine in Kittery Point. Although the company is the largest producer of recreational shells in America, it is still a family-owned business. Arthur Martin is president; his wife, Marjorie, is vice president; son Douglas designs for the firm; and son-in-law Ted Perry runs the manufacturing operation.

With its sturdy but lightweight construction, the Alden Ocean Shell is the most popular recreational shell, but Martin Marine also makes a double shell, an X-Oarcizer for year-round rowing, a Kittery skiff that you can assemble yourself, the Appledore Pod for rough water rowing, and the Martin Trainer for the serious rower. The Trainer combines the characteristics of an Alden Ocean Shell with a traditional racing shell, making it faster than the Alden but more stable than a true scull.

Prices for the Martin Marine boats start at $945.00 for the Kittery Skiff. The complete boat packages for the Alden Ocean Shells are $1595.00 for the single, and $2525.00 for the double. The double can be sold with a single rowing unit for $1805.00.

Write or call for more information or a price quotation on the boats and shipping charges. Hulls and oars are shipped freight collect. All other parts are shipped prepaid by UPS. Payment by MasterCard, Visa, check, or C.O.D.

MARTIN MARINE CO., INC.

The Montgomery Schoolhouse, Inc.

10 South Richford Road
Montgomery, Vermont 05470
(800) 533-TOYS (outside Vermont)
(802) 326-4272 (inside Vermont)

At The Montgomery Schoolhouse, a dedicated group of people are helping to build young imaginations by making wooden toys the way every parent would like them to be made: solid native pine and hard woods are designed, finished, and decorated with bright non-toxic colors, and are so durable that if a toy ever breaks, it will be repaired without charge.

The Montgomery Schoolhouse wooden toys are not only visually appealing, but also meet or exceed federal toy safety standards.

Most of the toys are designed for preschoolers, but they are loved by children of all ages. They are also collected by many for both decorative and nostalgic values. The Montgomery Schoolhouse selection of toys includes rattles, trucks, trains, cars, airplanes, alphabet blocks, and such all-time favorites as the Airplane Ride or the Bowling Elephant. The centerpiece for the collection, however, is the Double Decker Checker Bus™, a delightful toy that looks like a crowded English bus, but includes a checker board, and the passengers are the checkers!

The Montgomery Schoolhouse operates a retail shop at the plant.

Intermediates		*Midget Railway*™	
Fire Truck	$21.40	Engine	$4.10
Barrel Truck	14.50	Coal Car	3.60
Airplane Ride	32.50	Chocolate Pudding	3.60
Bowling Elephant™	49.50	*My Train*®	
Bumper Dumper™	22.50	Engine	13.60
Wood Play Blocks	27.00	Bottle Car	11.60
Midgets™		Caboose	11.60
Fire Truck	3.30	*Heirloom*™ *Rattles*	
Ambulance	3.30	Standard Bell	5.30
Air Taxi	3.30	Standard Disk	5.30

Free catalog. Wholesale available. No price quotes. Minimum order of $8.00. Product guaranteed. Goods stocked and shipped within two weeks by UPS or U.S. mail. Payment by MasterCard, Visa, check, or money order.

HC01 FIRE TRUCK   HC03 SCHOOL BUS   HC04 POLICE CAR   HC02 RESCUE VAN

New England Cheesemaking Supply

Box 85 Main Street
Ashfield, Massachusetts 01330
(413) 628-3808

Since 1978, New England Cheesemaking Supply has stocked a complete line of equipment for small scale dairy production, including cheese molds, cultures, books, presses, and cheese starter cultures for either the novice or professional cheesemaker. They also have equipment for making butter and yogurt.

With the Basic Cheese Kit, even a novice can save money while making additive and preservative-free cheeses. A more experienced cheesemaker, however, may want to invest in a Wheeler Cheese Press, hand-crafted in England from hard wood and stainless steel. Guaranteed to last a lifetime.

The Basic Cheese Kit is $19.95. New England Cheesemaking Supply also carries a kit for Fresh French Goat Cheese for $15.95, a Mozzarella Cheese Kit for $9.95, and a Coeur A La Creme Kit for $16.95. The cheese molds start at $4.50, and the starter cultures start at $4.00. They also carry Cheesecloth and wax, and a handy Off-the-Wall Press for $12.95.

A Home Milk Pasteurizer is available for $125.00, and the Wheeler Cheese Press is $169.95.

New England Cheesemaking Supply operates a retail outlet on premises. It is open daily from 8:00 A.M. to 4:00 P.M.

Catalog available for $1.00. Wholesale available. Products guaranteed. Goods stocked and shipped UPS or U.S. mail within 2-4 weeks. Will ship to Canada. Payment by MasterCard, Visa, check, or money order.

Making Yogurt

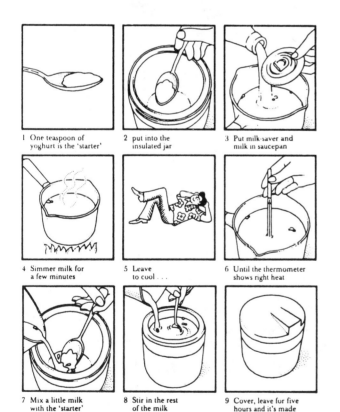

1 One teaspoon of yoghurt is the 'starter'
2 put into the insulated jar
3 Put milk-saver and milk in saucepan
4 Simmer milk for a few minutes
5 Leave to cool . . .
6 Until the thermometer shows right heat
7 Mix a little milk with the 'starter'
8 Stir in the rest of the milk
9 Cover, leave for five hours and it's made

> ***The Cheesemaker's Journal***
> *The Cheesemaker's Journal, the foremost publication in the country on specialty and handcrafted cheeses and cheesemakers, is not connected with New England Cheesemaking Supply, but is also located in Ashfield. Filled with articles and recipes for those who wish to try their hand at making dairy products at home, it has a worldwide circulation and often contains articles on specialty cheese and other dairy products from around the world. A six-issue subscription is $12.00.*

North Island Designs

2 Main Street
North Haven, Maine 04853
(800) 548-5648 (outside Maine)
(207) 867-2004 (inside Maine)

A rugged coastline, blue-green spruce, fields of wildflowers dotted with grazing sheep, sailboats crossing the bay are all images of island life reflected in the patterns of sweater kits created by North Island Design. Knitting kits, pattern books, wool yarns, and knitting accessories are produced by this business conducted on an island of 400 year-round residents, twelve miles off the coast of Maine. North Island is serviced by a nine-car ferry, has the smallest K-12 school in the state, and is surrounded by incredible natural beauty in all seasons.

The knitting kits contain everything the knitter needs—pattern, graph, natural fiber yarns, photo, buttons, and a label—to create a classic design that will be cherished by the wearer for years to come. The pattern books present several designs, stunning photographs of the finished sweaters, and island scenes, as well as the story of life on the island.

Prices for the standard line of sweater kits are $45.00 for a youth's pullover, $55.00 for an adult pullover, and $59.00 for an adult cardigan. Specialty

kits, such as the lobster boat pattern, range from $65.00 to $69.00. Kits are also available for vests, and children's pullovers and cardigans. The *Maine Island Classics* pattern book features twenty patterns for $14.95.

Catalog available for $2.00, refundable with purchase. Wholesale available. Price quotes by letter only. Products guaranteed. Goods stocked and shipped UPS or U.S. mail within one week. Will ship to Canada. Payment by MasterCard, Visa, check, or money order.

Sweater Patterns	Starry Night	Lobster Boat
Chickens	Island Spruce	Peasant Vest
Five Sheep	*Vest Patterns*	*Children's*
Appletree	Grazing Sheep	*Patterns*
Teddy Bear	Under the Apple	Schoolbus
Sailboat	Tree	Country Scene
Spring	Sunset over	City Scene
Fall	Camden Hills	The Farmyard
Cats	Sophisticated	Train at the
Lobster Boat	Chickens	Station

Rubber Stamps of America

P. O. Box 567-NEBM
Saxtons River, Vermont 05154
(802) 869-2622

A unique, unusual, and exclusive selection of hundreds of graphic rubber stamps. These high quality rubber stamps by New England artists such as Ken Brown, Jeanne Borofsky, Vivian Day, Susan Osgood, Ruth Kuetemeyer, John Kowalski, Anthony Toepfer, and Lisbeth Frolunde are designed for the stamping enthusiast as well as the casual stamper.

Hundreds of images are available, from wildlife to the wacky, each carefully crafted and guaranteed to create the best impression. They also carry several specialty items such as blank jigsaw puzzles, blank calendars for your own designs or for stamping.

The retail store is on Academy Avenue in Saxtons River, and is open Monday through Friday from 10:00 A.M. to 4:00 P.M., and on Saturday from 10:00 A.M. to 2:00 P.M.

Catalog $2.00, refundable with purchase. Wholesale available for resale only. All products are guaranteed. $10.00 minimum for credit card orders. Ships UPS and U.S. mail within 72 hours, except for custom orders to the United States and Canada. Maximum shipping time for custom orders is four weeks. Payment by MasterCard, Visa, check, or money order.

#351 $5.00

#285 $4.50

Bear Mail #537 $4.50

#673 $4.00

#330 $4.50

#135 $4.75

we've moved! #652 $4.75

#387 $4.75

#529 $4.75

Small Craft, Inc.

59 Brunswick Avenue
Moosup, Connecticut 06354
(203) 564-2751

The boats from Small Craft, Inc. are designed to meet the needs of the recreational rower: boats that are lightweight and that are sturdier, safer, and less expensive than professional rowing shells.

Boats from Small Craft are under 50 pounds fully rigged, except for their "Typhoon," which can be broken down into two easily carried units—a 45-pound hull and an 18-pound rig. Not only is a lighter boat easier to carry, it's faster in the water.

Small Craft boats are also safer. They are built with small-capacity, sealed cockpits. If the boat is flipped, it is easily righted with the rigger, and the cockpit comes up empty with no water in the hull. In addition, Small Craft offers a self-bailer option that keeps the cockpit draining under all conditions.

The skin of Small Craft shells are fully cored with syntactic foam, making them light, stiff, and able to float by themselves. If you were to rip a piece out of the boat and throw it in the water, it would float.

This fully cored skin, plus an additional three cubic feet expanded polystyrene foam "I-beam" that has been installed in the boat, means that the boat will maintain its shape and stiffness throughout the stroke.

Other design changes that Small Craft has made are geared toward making the boat more comfortable (they mounted the seat on skateboard wheels for a smoother movement), and faster (the maximum waterline beam is just aft of the riggers for greater stability and less loss of energy).

These new designs are only one part of Small Craft's dedication to continually improve the performance of recreational shells.

The Typhoon and Lightening models are recommended for beginners. The Typhoon lists for $1,395.00; the Lightening for $1,495.00. For the more experienced rower, the 266 Ocean Racer lists for $1,695.00 and the Racing Single for $1,995.00.

Free catalog. Wholesale available. Products guaranteed. Goods are stocked and shipped by common carrier F.O.B. Moosup, CT. Shipped within three weeks. Will ship to Canada. Payment by check or money order.

Stave Puzzles, Inc.

P. O. Box 329 R
Norwich, Vermont 05055
(802) 295-5200

Established in 1973, Stave Puzzles offers the world's most beautiful and creatively challenging puzzles. They have been featured on "Good Morning, America" and in the *Smithsonian* magazine. In 1988 they were used as a part of the commissioned White House Christmas decorations.

Stave Puzzles creates the only fine, handcut, mahogany-backed jigsaw puzzles being made today. In addition to traditional puzzles personalized for each order, they offer Limited Editions—hand-painted creations of exceptional beauty and puzzling challenge.

For instance, some of the Stave Puzzles unique creations can be assembled in more than one way . . . but only one is correct. "The Three Little Pigs" can be put together in 63 different ways. All the animals in the incredible "Noah's Ark" stand alone, yet interlock by holding hands, horns, flippers, tails, or tusks. The animals not only head for the ark two-by-two, but they are also in two layers, one of Stave puzzling tricks.

Stave's tricks have five levels of infuriating difficulty—their "Generation" puzzles. A "First Generation" has been personalized from existing art. A "Second Generation" is made using commissioned

art. A "Third Generation" puzzle is one in which the pieces fit into the puzzle in more than one way. A "Fourth Generation" puzzle fits together in several different ways. The "Fifth Generation" puzzles are based on a Möbius strip concept.

Stave Puzzles offers an incredible array from monochromatic wilderness silhouettes to folk and classical paintings. The 36-page catalog looks more like an art catalog than a list of puzzles. They will also create puzzles from your own design. Price range is $175 - $3,000. The "Three Little Pigs" puzzle is $695.00 and "Noah's Ark" is $1,595.00.

Their retail store is on Route 5 in Norwich, and is open Monday through Friday from 8:00 A.M. to 5:00 P.M. Appointments can be made for visiting the store at other times.

Catalog available for $10.00, refundable with purchase. Price quotes available by phone. Puzzles shipped by UPS, with delivery within six to eight weeks. Will ship to Canada. Payment by American Express, Visa, MasterCard.

Trow and Holden

P. O. Box 475
Barre, Vermont 05641
(800) 451-4349

Since Barre, Vermont, is the site of the world's largest granite quarry and the home for many of this country's best sculptors and stoneworkers, it is no surprise that it is also home to the company that manufactures the best tools for working in stone.

Since 1890, Trow and Holden has been making the highest quality power and hand tools for sculptors, masons, and other stoneworkers. It features specialty tools for splitting, shaping, carving, and finishing stone. It will also repair or retemper any of its tools.

All Trow and Holden tools are backed by 100 years of quality and precision, but it is the pneumatic carving tools that receive the most attention from their customers. These are designed as precision intruments to be used by artists and masons who specialize in such detailed work as repointing historic masonry.

The difference between the common chiseling tool used to remove mufflers and a Trow and Holden precision carving tool is deceptively simple. The Trow and Holden tool has neither retainer nor throttle, which allows the sculptor or mason to have greater control over the tool: one hand operates the tool as the other controls the chisel.

The chisel in a Trow and Holden tool has a round shank so that the chisel can be oriented independently of the tool, and the absence of the retainer means that the sculptor can pull the chisel away from the piston without any other action.

The pneumatic tools are available in a range of sizes, and the chisel blades can be purchased from Trow and Holden's existing stock of tempered, carbide tipped blades, or custom made to any length or width.

Prices on the pneumatic tools range from $258.50 for a Type-A short stroke tool to $639.50 for the Hand Facer. A ¾-B short stroke tool is $275.00, and a 1-HB short stroke is $285.00. Prices on the carbide tipped tools include ranges from $20.00 to $30.00 for the machine chisels; $25.00 to $45.00 for the marble chisels; and $18.00 to $30.00 for the carver's drills. All steel tools start at $8.00 for the machine chisels, $10.00 for the cleaning up chisels, and $15.00 for a ripper.

Trow and Holden operates a retail store at the site of their factory. Call for hours.

Free catalog. Wholesale available. Price quotes only on specialty items or custom-made tools, by phone or letter. Products guaranteed. Goods that are in stock are shipped within two weeks by UPS, U.S. mail, Federal Express, or Purolator. Will ship to Canada. Payment by MasterCard, Visa, check, or money order.

The Vermont Patchworks

Box 229
Shrewsbury, Vermont 05738
(800) 451-4044

The Vermont Patchworks is a mail order business specializing in products for the quilter. It offers a comprehensive selection of books and hard-to-find quilting supplies. There's even a selection of gifts for the quilter.

Among the specialty notions are imported English and Japanese needles, gold quilting needles, IBC silk pins, and a deerskin pioneer thimble. The Vermont Patchworks Sourcebook also lists a selection of drafting supplies; color and design aids; how-to and pattern books; books on color, design, and inspiration; and historical and reference books about quilting. They even have videos to help the novices as well as the expert quilters.

Catalog available for $2.00, refundable with purchase. Products guaranteed. Goods stocked and shipped by UPS or U.S. mail within 48 hours. Will ship to Canada. Payment by MasterCard, Visa, check, or money order.

Notions	
Imported English Needles	$ .95
"Majestic 88" Needle	3.25
IBC Quilting Pins	4.00
IBC Silk Pins	3.50
Drafting Supplies	
Quilt and Sew Ruler	4.50
Bow Compass	12.95
Color and Design Aids	
Pantone Color Selector	13.00
Arabic Allover Patterns	3.50
Books	
Quilts! Quilts! Quilts!	19.95
Cutting Up With Curves	21.95
Baltimore Beauties and Beyond	14.95
Lap Quilting	19.95
The Elements of Color	18.95
Pattern Design	5.95
Twentieth Century Quilts	22.95
Videos	
Palettes for Patchwork	29.95
A Video Guide to Quilting	32.00

Vermont Voyageur Equipment

Route 242, Box 1010
Montgomery Center, Vermont 05471
(802) 326-4789

On Vermont's Route 242, in the shadow of Jay Peak, Vermont Voyageur Equipment designs and manufactures its own line of expedition-quality outdoor clothing and equipment. It is a family business owned by Sharon and Rolf Anderson.

The Andersons conduct extensive research and field tests of all their equipment. They even admit that they have made clothes and equipment in the past that, although better than most mass-produced products, were still not as sturdy or water repellent as they wanted.

"We searched a long time for the very best quality nylon taffeta for our Wind River Anorak™. Many suppliers offered us what the big-name companies use—low-quality nylon that needs a light coating to be windproof. This results in a lot of condensation in a jacket that should be breathable. Finally, we found a small American company that could sell us the highest-quality nylon taffeta: an extremely strong, tightly woven fabric which is very windproof without sacrificing breathability."

The Andersons use that same high-quality nylon taffeta in their Wind River Pants, and they demand the same quality for all of their products. They developed a rugged tarp and hammock set that provides maximum warmth and comfort while allowing camping with little or no damage to the landscape.

One of the highlights of the Voyageur product line is the manufactured version of the Peter Limmer & Sons, Inc., custom handcrafted boot. The Limmer Hiking Boot is famous for its durability and comfort. The uppers are made from one piece of leather and have a Norwegian welt sole attachment. This results in a minimum of exposed stitching and ensures a waterproof boot. Despite the growing number of commercial boot manufacturers, Peter Limmer & Sons has a devoted following, and many hikers and backpackers refuse to wear anything but a Limmer boot.

The Limmer Hiking Boots are available for $150.00. Prices for other items range from $10.50 for a Voyageur Duffel Bag™ and $39.00 for a pair of Wind River Pants™ to $75.00 for a Gale River Parka™ and $98.00 for a Voyageur Rain Tarp™.

"The Limmer Hiking Boot may be the best boot value in the world."
—BACKPACKER Magazine

Vermont Voyageur operates two retail shops in addition to their mail order business. One is at the Hazen's Notch X-C Ski Area on Route 58 in Montgomery Center, and is open seven days a week from December to April. Hours are from 9:00 A.M. to 5:00 P.M. A second shop is on Route 242 in Montgomery Center and is open seven days a week all year round, 9:00 A.M. to 5:00 P.M.

Free catalog. Products guaranteed. Most goods stocked, some made to order. Ships UPS unless otherwise requested, within three weeks. Customer will be notified if shipping time is extended. Will ship to Canada. No telephone orders. Payment by check or money order.

WoodenBoat School

P. O. Box 78
Naskeag Road
Brookline, Maine 04616
(207) 359-4651

Ten years ago, on 60-acres of a "gentleman's saltwater farm" on the coast of Maine's Eggemoggin Reach, a group of people decided to start a school that would teach boatbuilding.

Today that school offers more than thirty-five courses between June and October. Most classes last one week, although some, such as Fundamentals of Boatbuilding, extend over two weeks.

Almost 500 students attend the school each summer to learn to build dories, canoes, kayaks, iceboats, and construction models. They represent a diverse mix of personalities, lifestyles, and interests. The one thing they have in common is an interest in boatbuilding and a love of the sea. If you share this love and would like to spend a week or more learning more, call or write for a catalog. Courses start in mid-June. Tuition for the 1990 courses started at $390.00. All courses may not be offered every year.

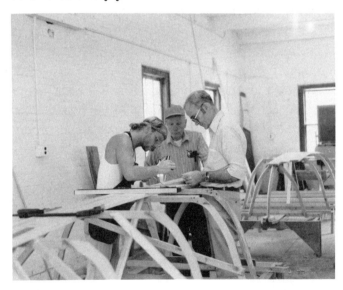

1990 Courses	
Fundamentals of Boatbuilding	Building Half Models
Lofting	Building Construction
Building the Haven 12½	Models
Building a Dory	Basic Woodworking
Wood/Epoxy Boatbuilding	Marine Carving
Stitch-and-Glue Boatbuilding	Advanced Carving and
Building Your Own	Patternmaking
DK-14 Kayak	Marine Surveying
Building the Nutshell	Marine Mechanics
Pram Kit	Fiberglass Engineering
Building the Friendship	and Surveying
Sloop	Marine Painting
Joinerwork	and Varnishing
Wooden Boat	Sailmaking
Repair Methods	Boat Design
Runabout Repair & Restoration	Marine Photography
Instant Boats	Drawing and Painting
Iceboat Construction	Elements of Seamanship
Loft and Build a Canoe Mold	Coastwise Navigation
Building the Maine	Celestial Navigation
Guide Canoe	Craft of Sail
Canoe Repair & Restoration	Cruising Boat Seamanship

Zone VI Studios

708 Elm Street
Newfane, Vermont 05345
(802) 257-5161

In 1972, Fred Picker started Zone VI Studios in his garage, offering the best equipment for photographers who work in a black-and-white 4" x 5" format. Over the next fifteen years, Zone VI grew from one person to twelve, and Fred's business continues to grow, mainly due to the philosophy of offering only the best products and the best values, giving the best possible customer service, and treating people with the respect they deserve.

Zone VI doesn't stock a lot of different brands of similar items because it wants to offer only the best. And when the best item available is not good enough for Zone VI, it makes its own. Zone VI produces one of the finest 4 x 5 wooden field cameras ever built— a camera assembled from parts made in Vermont. It also makes its own cold lights, wooden tripods, and imports printing paper made in France to Zone VI's specifications.

The staff at Zone VI can answer questions about the products or anything at all to do with photography. Perhaps this explains why many of their customers have been loyal to Zone VI since Fred was shipping the equipment out of his garage. Zone VI works hard to please customers, not only with the quality of the products, but with the service provided.

Free catalog. All products carry a 30-day money-back guarantee and have a lifetime repair or replacement guarantee. Goods stocked and shipped UPS or U.S. mail within one or two days. Will ship worldwide. Payment by American Express, MasterCard, Visa, Discover, check, or money order.

Zone VI 4 x 5 Camera	$1,185.00
Complete One-Lens 4 x 5 Outfit	1,925.00
Zone VI Archival Print Washer	375.00
Zone VI Standard Wooden Tripod	297.00
Electronic Static Brush	245.00
25 Sheets 8 x 10 Printing Paper	19.00
100 Sheets 8 x 10 Printing Paper	59.00

Zone IV Print Critique

Send up to six prints, unmounted 8 x 10 (or smaller), along with your check for $100.00 payable to either The Sierra Club Foundation, Inc., Friends of the Earth Foundation, Inc., or The Wilderness Society Foundation, Inc. (All are tax deductible.) Lil Farber and Fred Picker will write their impressions of your work, make suggestions and answer your questions.

ADVENTURES IN NEW ENGLAND

TRAVEL OPPORTUNITES AND UNIQUE VACATIONS

Balloon Sports

145 Glenwood Avenue
Portland, Maine 04103
(207) 772-4401

I magine floating in the gentle air currents over the natural splendor of southern Maine, viewing the panorama of Sebago Lake, Casco Bay's Calendar Islands, or snow-capped Mount Washington. This could be the most unique adventure of your lifetime.

Suspended from a pillow of air, whisked away in a wicker perch, when you are flying in the modern hot air balloon you are flying in basically the same aircraft that the Montgo-flier brothers developed 200 years ago. Air heated by the propane burner gives the balloon life, and wind dictates the speed and direction of the voyage. Tom and Migs Handcock, the chief aeronauts of Balloon Sports, Maine's oldest balloon voyage company, fly every day of the year.

The balloons accommodate six passengers and each flight lasts about one hour. The whole event takes approximately three to four hours from set-up to the return to your car. Friends are welcome to come along and ride in the chase vehicle.

Each flight ends with the French tradition of a champagne toast and a snack.

All pilots and equipment are regulated and tested by the Federal Aviation Administration. Flights are $125.00 per person. Balloon Sports requires a non-refundable $75 deposit per person. If weather prevents the balloon from going up, your time will be rescheduled.

...leave the world behind and create some of the magical memories that only a balloon ride can provide.

Balloon Sports also offers gift certificates. What better gift than to a chance to leave the world behind and create some of the magical memories that only a balloon ride can provide?

Free brochure. Price quotes by letter or phone. Payment by MasterCard or Visa.

Captain John's Sport Fishing Center, Inc.

15 First Street
Waterford, Connecticut 06385
(203) 443-7259

One of the pioneers of sport fishing was Captain Earle Wadsworth, who founded a family-owned business that has been in operation for three generations.

Today, the family tradition is carried on by Captain John Wadsworth, who started some of the first Nature Cruises, carrying passengers to watch whales, bald eagles, and harbor seals in their natural habitat. All Nature Cruises take place on one of Captain John's four Sunbeam Express boats. The bald eagle watches occur from January to mid-March, harbor seals are most abundant in March and April, and whale watches sail May to September. A naturalist from the Mystic Marinelife Aquarium is on board for every trip to answer any questions you might have.

The Sport Fishing Center was also one of the first to start long range Open Boat Tuna Fish Trips to the continental shelf on two-, three-, or four-day trips. From late fall through spring, they offer open boat cod

fishing, and tuna, marlin, swordfish, and shark fishing excursions during the summer and fall. Private charters can be arranged.

The third generation, Captain Bob Wadsworth, oversees the fleet of boats in their home port on the Niantic River. With boats ranging in size from 26' to 100', they have a cruise to fit your needs whether you want to make a record-breaking catch or simply capture on film nature's beautiful mammals and wildlife in their native environment.

The cruises to watch the bald eagles or harbor seals sail every Sunday. The cost for adults is $20.00. Whale-watching cruises sail on Sunday and Thursday. The cost for adults is $30.00.

Prices for the fishing charters vary from $35.00 for a one-day excursion for flounder to $520.00 for a four-day excursion for tuna and shark. Private charters are available.

Call or write for a free brochure.

Harbor Seals

Coastwise Packet Company

Box 429
Vineyard Haven, Massachusetts 02568
(508) 693-1699

Perhaps no other coastal region in the world is so handsomely endowed with all the elements that produce the finest sailing and cruising conditions as the waters around Cape Cod. Prevailing westerly winds provide dependable breezes, and harbors once crowded with tall ships still contain unforgettable ports-of-call with sandy beaches, granite wharves, and white-trimmed houses.

Shenandoah sails in the wake of those tall ships, cruising the waters of Nantucket, Vineyard, Block Island, and Long Island sounds. The only square-rigged topsail clipper schooner in the business and the only windjammer cruise service in operation on the Rhode Island and Massachusetts coast, *Shenandoah* is a 152-foot schooner built expressly for passen-

ger service and with an adherence to mid-nineteenth century practices of putting together and outfitting a sizeable sailing ship.

Shenandoah's home port is Vineyard Haven, but she sails between Nantucket and Long Island. Cruises are scheduled from the middle of June through the middle of September. She leaves Vineyard Haven each Monday morning and returns Saturday afternoon, following no pre-set route. Guided by wind and tide, each evening—weather permitting—will find her anchored in a different harbor.

The finest Yankee fare is served daily and will satisfy the heartiest seagoing appetite.

At $600.00 per person, it is an affordable way to capture a bit of the past, to experience a part of our American heritage.

Free brochure. Payment by personal check or cash only. Advance deposit of $200.00 per person required. Reduced rates for groups available.

Cycle Inn/Walking Inn Vermont, Inc.

P. O. Box 243-NEBM
Ludlow, Vermont 05149-0243
(802) 228-8799

Two innkeepers in Ludlow, Vermont, have created an attractive variation of the organized cycling tour and for those who prefer a more personalized, private vacation. Ron Perry, proprietor of the Okemo Inn, and Ruth Combes of the Combes Family Inn, noticed that many of their summer guests were from tour groups who had returned to retrace the tour at a slower pace. Ron and Ruth formed Cycle Inn Vermont and Walking Inn Vermont to provide an option for those who prefer an excursion at a slower pace, away from the open roads.

The Cycling and Walking Tours range from two days to a week or longer, depending on your ambition and ability. You choose the inns you wish to visit and the number of miles you feel you can travel each day. Each innkeeper greets you with cozy, comfortable lodging and a delicious homecooked meal. Your luggage and other personal belongings are transported from inn to inn, leaving you free to enjoy the pleasures of the Vermont countryside.

For cyclists, these pleasures can be the challenge of the mountainous terrain, the enchantment of a winding river valley, or the charm of historic country villages. For walkers, untraveled back roads may reveal swimming holes, luscious lakes or mountain

Photo by Paul O. Boisvert

streams, indigenous wild flowers, intriguing cemeteries, charming villages, and—often the favorite for many visitors—Vermont's abundant wildlife. Each day ends with the New England hospitality of an historic country inn.

The touring season starts in late spring and extends through October. Reservations should be made at least ten days in advance. Call or write for a free brochure. Most tours cost approximately $85.00 per person per day, which includes lodging, breakfast and dinner, taxes and gratuities. Bicycle and helmet rentals available.

Mystic River Balloon Adventures

17 Carriage Drive
Stonington, Connecticut 06378
(203) 535-0283

Gilbert Foster, the aeronaut of Mystic River Balloon Adventures, has flown his balloon all over the world. He has drifted over the dramatic Swiss Alps and Berkshire mountains, the expansive lands of Australia, the cornfields of Iowa, the green farmlands of Kentucky and Tennessee, and the busy city of Boston.

But he believes the Mystic/Stonington area is the most exciting and beautiful area for the occasional balloonist. Here is a picturesque blend of farms, woods, streams, ponds, hills, and the charming inlets and harbors of Long Island Sound.

Gilbert offers flights for individuals, parties, or promotions beginning in May of each year, although his busiest time is summer and when the fall foliage is in full color. Flights are scheduled for early morning or late afternoon, and last approximately one hour. Landings are celebrated with champagne or sparkling cider, some instant pictures, and a certificate to document the occasion.

Although Gilbert provides the instant pictures, feel free to bring your own still camera and plenty of film. Although no video equipment is allowed the photographic opportunities are endless as you float over a misty summer landscape or brilliant fall display.

Flights are $225.00 per person. A minimum of two people is required on flights reserved for Monday through Friday. A 50 percent deposit is required to hold your reservation. Deposits must be received within seven days of your booking. Prepaid gift certificates are available and may be ordered at any time. If a flight is cancelled due to weather conditions, alternate bookings can be scheduled, often the next day.

Call or write for more information.

New England Bicycle Tours

P. O. Box 26-M
Randolph, Vermont 05060
(800) 233-2128

New England Bicycle Tours offers the elegance of Victorian New England, the spectacular highlights of historical villages, fall foliage unsurpassed by any other region of the country, and the time to enjoy it all at the speed of a coasting bicycle.

Personal attention and small touring groups have made the vacations offered by New England Bicycle Tours a pleasing and growing success. The people who run NEBT are bicyclists through and through and know what it takes to make a truly special bicycle vacation, whether it's a weekend jaunt, a week-long exploration, a longer summer trip to Europe, or a winter tour of the Caribbean.

Their weekend tours are usually based at one of New England's historic inns, where you can sleep in comfort only moments away from the most scenic landscapes in New England. Their most popular tour is based at The Vermont Marble Inn in Fair Haven, and visits Dorset, Middletown Springs, and the exquisite scenery in the heart of Vermont's western lake district.

The Woodstock Weekend visits some of the state's most lovingly preserved towns, such as Plymouth and Barnard, and ends each day with a stay at the Kedron Valley Inn, a 150-year-old monument to graceful hospitality nestled in the heart of Vermont's horse country.

The cycling on the Wallingford Weekend tour passes quiet villages and Wilson's Castle, a spectacular architectural masterpiece housing a unique collection of European furniture and art, and ends at the Wallingford Inn, a charming Victorian mansion built in 1876.

The other weekend tours include trips along the Black and Saxtons rivers, and a "fat-tire" weekend at the Stratton Mountain resort.

The five-day vacations include a Cape Islands trip that starts at Woods Hole, Massachusetts and travels to Martha's Vineyard and Nantucket, exploring the coves and quiet towns, dining on some of the finest New England food, sleeping in the restored splendor of the Admiral Benbow Inn or the Stumble Inne.

Other five-day tours cover the western lake district or the historic area surrounding Woodstock. New England Bicycle Tours also offers summer trips to Sweden and winter trips to the Caribbean. Or they will custom design a trip around whatever adventure you want your vacation to include.

Free catalog with discounts to travel agents and groups of 15 or more. Price quotes for custom tours only. Payment by MasterCard, Visa, check, money order.

New England Whitewater Center

P. O. Box 21
Caratunk, Maine 04925
(800) 766-7238 (outside Maine)
(207) 775-2345

The magic of New England's summers, so it has been said, lies in its rivers—those warm, fast-flowing mountain streams that spark the imagination and offer the challenge of riding the river rapids.

Since 1982 the licensed guides of New England Whitewater Center have been taking rafters into the wilderness to face the Kennebec, Dead, and Penobscot rivers. Their trips offer a first-time novice a pleasant excursion with opportunities to build rafting skills while enjoying the enchanting Maine scenery and abundant wildlife. The experienced wilderness sportsman can take part in a thrilling run down a narrow mountain gorge where the waters flow deep and fast.

After each day's magic, rafters can relax and trade stories at one of the three lodgings owned by the Center: the nineteenth-century Sterling Inn Bed & Breakfast, the Marshall's Hotel, or cabins along the river. Camping is also available. In addition, the Center offers trips that include canoeing, kayaking, and boardsailing.

New England Whitewater Center

Because the Center is a full-capacity, year-round company, it also hosts snowmobilers, skiers, hikers, mountain bikers, and tourists. The Center is only two hours from Portland, and is the perfect year-round vacation spot.

Prices for weekend trips on either Penobscot or Dead rivers start at $228 per person for double occupancy at the Marshall Hotel, $236 per person for the Center's cabins or Sterling Inn.

Free catalog. Price quotes by letter or mail. Payment by MasterCard, Visa, check, or money order.

The Sterling Inn

North Woods Ways

P. O. Box 286
Dover-Foxcroft, Maine 04426
(207) 564-3032

Since they were children, Garrett and Alexandra Conover have been exploring the woods and paddling the rivers of Maine, and in 1980 they turned that interest into a profession. After extended apprenticeships with renowned Maine guide "Mick Fahey," they formed North Woods Ways, in part from a strong wish to carry on the heritage of the Maine guide. North Woods Ways is currently based at the North Woods Arts Center, a non-profit school dedicated to the research, teaching, and application of traditional north woods skills.

> *"This is the most personable and professional guiding service in Maine."*
>
> —Bill Curtsinger,
> *contract photographer,*
> National Geographic

But you don't have to have the skills of a Maine guide to follow Garrett and Alexandra into the north woods. They offer five- to fourteen-day canoe trips for both beginning and experienced canoeists. Their trips combine woods and water skills, natural history, and aspects of human uses of wildlands. The emphasis on each of these elements is adjusted to meet the interests of each group of travelers.

The extensive experience of Alexandra and Garrett ensure that each trip is comfortable and relaxing with plenty of time for exploration, and the enjoyment of each individual's wilderness experience.

North Woods Ways provides canoes, paddles, life vests, gear, cook set, food, and shelter. They will suggest a list of personal gear and equipment.

North Woods Ways operates year-round. During the spring, summer, and fall trips are available on the St. John, Moose, Penobscot, Allagash, and St. Croix rivers, and into the Labrador wilderness. During the winter, a switch to snowshoes and toboggans allows exploration of the frozen waterways of Maine, Minnesota, and much of the Canadian north.

They also offer a slide and lecture series with several different programs that combine Garrett's skills as an outdoor expert, storyteller, and photographer.

Call or write for a free brochure about either the trips or the lecture series.

NORTH WOODS WAYS

Northern Outdoors

Route 201
P. O. Box 100
The Forks, Maine 04985
(207) 663-4466
(800) 765-7238

The Northeast's most successful outdoor adventure resort company sets the standards by which others are judged. The first-class amenities and wide range of programs provide something for everyone from the veteran river runner to the novice woodsman who wants to explore the wilds of Maine.

Begun in 1976 with a second-hand raft, truck, and trailer, Northern Outdoors has opened resort centers that offer a variety of adventures and facilities.

From April to October, Northern Outdoors schedules rafting trips on the Kennebec, Dead, and Penobscot rivers. They provide everything—guides, equipment, even a riverside steak cookout. The base lodges have deluxe accommodations, and the Kennebec Lodge features a restaurant, bar, swimming pool, hot tub, sauna, and platform tennis.

Tours can be arranged for individuals or groups. Additional programs include trips for hunting, snowmobiling, mountain biking, kayaking, bass fishing, rafting, horseback riding, and various combinations. They even have a "Landlubbers Package" for partners of the adventurers who wish to share only in the nighttime fun.

For the folks of Northern Outdoors, this is not just a business—it's a way of life. And they want to share their love of the outdoors with you.

A one-day Kennebec rafting adventure starts at $75.00 per person during the week and $90.00 on weekends. With an added mini-vacation (two nights, dinner, two breakfasts, and use of resort facilities), prices start at $119.00 for camping, $133.00 for use of a cabin, and $155.00 for use of a lodge. Horseback adventures start at $45.00 per person and mountain bike tours start at $60.00.

Free catalog. Price quotes by letter or phone. Payment by MasterCard or Visa.

Saco Bound/Downeast Whitewater Rafting Company

P. O. Box 119T
Center Conway, New Hampshire 03813
(603) 447-2177 or 3801 (Saco Bound)
(603) 447-3002 or 3801 (Downeast Whitewater)

Started in 1979, Saco Bound/Downeast Whitewater tries to offer a wilderness trip for any level of interest and experience. Saco Bound specializes in peaceful, scenic canoe trips on the Saco River, where cool, crystal-clear waters gently flow over a white sand bottom flanked by miles of beaches—perfect for short excursions or overnight camping.

If you're more adventurous, try the Downeast Whitewater trips on the Kennebec, Penobscot, or Dead rivers. An exciting ride down some of the best river rapids in the country can be followed by a peaceful stay at the Kelley Brook Resort or the Dew Drop Inn. Or try the "2 Days, 2 Rivers" trip that covers rafting on both the Penobscot and Kennebec, the Penobscot-Squaw Mountain at Moosehead Resort Package, or the Kennebec-Sugarloaf Inn Resort Package.

The helpful staff are all expert river people with years of experience. A full transportation service is available for those renting or using their own canoe.

The season starts in April and ends in October. All rafting trips are on dam-controlled rivers with Class IV and V whitewater. They operate daily all season. Prices start at $20.00 per person for a one-day trip on the Saco, which includes a seven- or eleven-mile trip with stops for swimming, sunning, and picnicking.

Prices for overnight rafting trips on the Kennnebec start at $110.00 per person for a camping site, two nights, two breakfasts, one dinner, and a river lunch. A trip with overnight lodging at the Dew Drop Inn starts at $147.00 per person. A trip with a two-night stay at Squaw Mountain Resort starts at $157.00 per person. Prices do not include equipment rental.

Call or write for free brochure. Price quotes for groups and special trips by telephone. Payment by Master-Card, Visa, check, or money order.

Saco Bound Downeast
RIVER OUTFITTERS
Whitewater Rafting
Kayak & Canoe School
Saco River Canoe Trips

Schooner Captains

Box 482-TE
Rockland, Maine 04841
(207) 594-8007
(800) 648-4544 (outside Maine)

Schooner Captains is a group of four independently owned and operated schooners providing three-day and six-day windjammer cruises along the coast of Maine. The schooners *Heritage, Isaac H. Evans, Lewis R. French*, and *American Eagle* are traditional wooden crafts that take passengers for an unforgettable trip along the Maine coast, exploring granite islands or spending a leisurely day sunning in a remote harbor.

You can take a turn at the wheel, help raise the sails, or row one of the dinghies ashore for a clambake or lobster feast. A perfect getaway to another world—no phones, no television or mail, not even an engine to spoil the perfect blend of sea, sky, and wind.

The sailing season for Schooner Captains is from late May to early October. All ships are inspected annually by the U.S. Coast Guard; all captains are licensed. A deposit of $150.00 per person is required. Trips starts at $440.00 per person.

Call or write for a free brochure. Payment by Master-Card, Visa, check, or cash.

Spirit of Ethan Allen

Green Mountain Boat Lines, Ltd.
P. O. Box 2033
South Burlington, Vermont 05403
(802) 862-8300 (office)
(802) 862-9685 (for reservations and information)

Did you know that Vermont has its own Loch Ness Monster? He's Champ, first sighted in Lake Champlain in 1609. The single sighting by the most people of the "reptilian serpent" occurred in 1984 when 70 passengers on the deck of the cruise ship *Spirit of Ethan Allen* all spotted Champ swimming alongside the boat.

But don't just come for the monster. Vermont's largest dinner excursion boat is a refurbished paddlewheeler that features a variety of cruises to entertain and inform. The romantic atmosphere of the Captain's Dinner Cruise and the Sunset Cruise provide a delightful change of pace from the average evening out.

The star outing, however, is the Scenic Narrated Cruise, which is filled with tales of fierce naval battles,

regional lore, and little known names and places to go along with the unforgettable Vermont scenery. As the boat slowly cruises Lake Champlain from Burlington, Vermont, Captain Frank Shea tells about the lake and the region around it, from its discovery in 1609 by Samuel de Champlain to the 1984 sighting of Champ.

He'll tell you about the Shelburne Shipyard, the oldest continually-operating shipyard in the country. He'll talk about the Champlain Thrust, a pre-Cambrian geological fault unlike any other in the world. He knows about the naval battles in which Benedict Arnold participated, and how Ethan Allen's seige of Fort Ticonderoga left a lasting mark on the lake. He'll even point out the rock formation that the British mistook for an American ship and spent a day trying to sink.

Stroll topside for sun and fresh air. If it's a cool or rainy day, the cruise takes on a mystical aura. Comfort is maintained with the fully enclosed and heated lower deck and a quickly enclosed upper deck.

Don't come just for the monster, but don't be surprised if you look over the rail and spot a strange reptilian hump traveling alongside the boat.

Arrange for your cruise by mail or phone and join Captain Frank Shea for a trip along the "west coast of New England."

Payment by MasterCard or Visa.

Voyagers Whitewater

Route 201
The Forks, Maine 04985
(207) 663-4423

Competition among rafting companies in Maine is fierce, with each company trying to offer something unique. In 1981 John P. Kokajko felt he had discovered something that was missing from the other companies: trips with small groups of people.

"After guiding for another company for three years, I realized two things. One was that the small trips are more fun. On a small trip everyone gets to know each other better. The second was that as long as the trip size was small, I would enjoy guiding for a very long time. So I started Voyagers Whitewater to run small trips. They are more fun for you and for us."

The high levels of personal fun, playfulness, and river-running skills are maintained by providing a ratio of four customers to one guide. The Voyagers trips run the Kennebec, Dead, or the West Branch of the Penobscot in some of the most exciting waters in the country. And if you're game enough to try their sportrafting trips, you can learn to play the river, using the skill of the guide and the paddling of the crew.

Another specialty offered on each trip is the gourmet cooking of Susan Varney, who spent two years as a chef in a French restaurant, and follows her mother's tradition of gathering and serving wild edibles. Each day's rafting may end with a meal of fiddlehead quiche, duck with elderberry sauce, steak, or fresh Maine trout. The meal is topped off with a luscious homemade dessert such as chocolate mousse or peach cobbler.

Personal attention is the trademark of Voyagers Whitewater, and Susan and John are just waiting to take you on an unforgettable trip.

Call or write for free information. Voyagers provides guides, rafts, helmets, life jackets, and paddles. Trips are scheduled from May to October and start at approximately $80.00 per person. Group rates are available. Call or write for a full price list.

Yankee Schooner Cruises

P. O. Box 696X
Camden, Maine 04843
(800) 255-4449
(207) 236-4449

Down East Maine is a special place—a rugged, hilly coast of rock and pine, deeply indented by bays and rivers, and protected by thousands of islands. Here you can explore coastal villages, deserted islands, and quiet coves shared only with the seals. There is a magnificent beauty here found nowhere else on earth. It is one of the world's greatest sailing areas.

The majestic tall ships of Yankee Schooner Cruises make the experience of sailing Down East available to anyone who wants to join a group of adventurers for a three- or six-day cruise. Help sail the ship, row the longboat to shore, or learn to navigate. You'll enjoy the Down East down home food, and you'll never forget the thrill of sailing a fully rigged schooner.

There is no set itinerary. Each day's favorable wind may sail you to a secluded cove or the harbor of a coastal fishing village.

Relax and rejuvenate with the cruising lifestyle.

Enjoy the teeming Maine wildlife along the coast while the experienced captain and crew devote themselves to making your adventure memorable.

The schooner *Roseway* is 137 feet long and is U.S. Coast Guard inspected and certified. The ship, the last active pilot schooner in the United States, was refitted with all the modern amenities, and can accommodate special charters as well as the individual sailor. The *Roseway* also sails a winter schedule of cruises in the Virgin Islands.

The *Roseway* sails out of Sharp's Wharf, Camden each Monday and returns by Saturday noon. A $200.00 deposit per person is required. Most cruises start at $525.00 per person. Private charters are available.

Free catalog. Payment by MasterCard, Visa, check, or money order.

Photos by Bill Putnam

THE UNUSUAL AND THE UNIQUE

LET'S NOT FORGET ANYBODY

Acadia Publishing Company

P. O. Box 170
Bar Harbor, Maine 04609
(207) 288-9025

Acadia Publishing specializes in quality books with a Maine/New England theme, and is the largest producer of books, guides, and informative literature on Acadia National Park and the Bar Harbor area. They also offer guides for motorists, hikers, and even a book entitled *Lobsters, Inside—Out*, the only authoritative book on that fascinating crustacean.

Acadia operates a retail shop in Hulls Cove in Bar Harbor that is open daily from 8:00 A.M. to 4:30 P.M.

ACADIA PUBLISHING COMPANY

Catalog available for $1.00, refundable with purchase. Wholesale available; no price quotes. Goods stocked and shipped by UPS or U.S. mail within two weeks. Will ship to Canada. Products guaranteed. Payment by check or money order.

Books

The Lost Tales of Horatio Alger, edited by Gary Scharnhorst. $21.95.

The Eloquent Edge: 15 Maine Women Writers, edited by Kathleen Lignell and Margery Wilson. $21.95.

Discovering Acadia: A Guide for Young Naturalists, by Margaret Scheid. Children's. $11.95.

Dabbler and the Purple Cup, by Dale Leroux. Children's. $15.95.

My Dear Sarah Anne: Letters from a Century Ago, by Teisha Smedstad. $15.95.

Growing Up Summer, By Marjorie Whittlesey. Juvenile. $6.95.

Fair Play, by L. J. Harwood. Young Adult. $6.95.

A Romance of Mount Desert, by A. A. Hayes. $8.95

John Gilley, One of the Forgotten Millions, by Charles W. Eliot. $3.95.

Lobsters Inside—Out, by Robert and Juanita Bayer. $3.95.

The Story of Acadia National Park, by George B. Dorr. $7.95.

The Motorists Guide to Acadia National Park and Mount Desert Island. $2.95

A Hiking Guide to Acadia National Park and Mount Desert Island, by Robert Moran. $2.25.

Acadia National Park Coloring Book, by April and Robert Moran. Children's. $2.50.

Videos

Portrait of an Island (Mount Desert). $19.95.

Autumn in Acadia. $14.95.

Return to the Wild. $15.95.

Maps

America Claimed by France, 18th Century. $7.95.

Historical Map of Mount Desert Island. $7.95

Arts and Flowers of Cider Hill Farm

RR #1, Box 1066-NE
Windsor, Vermont 05089-9728
(802) 674-5293

Gary Milek is a nationally recognized artist who is well-known for his intimate and detailed egg tempra landscapes. His art has been exhibited throughout New England, and in New York City, Washington, DC, and California. In 1987 he was honored with a one-man show at St. Gaudens National Historic Site, Cornish, New Hampshire, and in October 1987 *American Artist* magazine did an extensive article about his work.

Sarah Milek is an herbalist. She grows herbs and everlastings, produces herbal products, wreaths, and bouquets, teaches, and designs flower arrangements for interior designers and weddings.

Several years ago, Sarah was preparing a presentation on everlastings and asked Gary to draw several sketches of her flowers. The presentation was a success. After the lecture, she had many requests for posters of Gary's art. The idea for Arts and Flowers of Cider Hill Farm was born.

Together Sarah and Gary have produced a series of attractive paintings, among them a garden of culinary herbs, an arrangement of wedding herbs, and a profusion of wildflowers. Their goal is to produce beautiful horticultural prints inspired by their gardens. They are committed to keeping in touch with nature through their gardens, paintings, herbs, and flowers.

They will sell you a print through the mail or at their farm. If you go to the farm, don't forget to ask for a tour of the gardens.

Catalog available for $2.00, which includes a set of sample note cards and a price list of the larger prints. Wholesale available. Goods are stocked, with custom framing available. Prints and cards are shipped UPS within two weeks; four if framing is requested. Framed prints are shipped F.O.B. Windsor, Vermont. Will ship to Canada. Payment by MasterCard, Visa, check, or money order.

Prints	Rolled in Tube	Flat With Shrink Wrap
Culinary Herbs	$ 22.00	$ 31.00
Wedding Herbs	20.00	25.00
Rosemary	25.00	30.00
New England Wildflowers	40.00	48.00
Black Raspberries	55.00	63.00
Alpine Strawberries	15.00	30.00
Delphiniums	110.00	122.00
Digitalis (Foxgloves)	120.00	132.00
Dry Flowers and Potpourri		
Wedding Herbs Basket	$30.00	
Wedding Herbs Potpourri	7.00	
Strewing Herbs	20.00	

Beacon Bills

228 Main Street
Bar Harbor, Maine 04609
(207) 288-9908

A working harbor, an old-run down sardine cannery, a lobster shack, and lighthouses on rocky cliffs keeping watch over the sea are all traditional scenes of the Maine coastline that have been captured in pen and ink by Wayne Edmondson and are

sold by Beacon Bills. They have been carefully rendered using a stippling technique that results in fine detail as well as halftones and shadows.

Reproduced at the same size as the original work, these 6½" x 9" signed prints are available both matted and unmatted. A matted print will fit a standard 11" x 14" frame. Beacon Bills' note cards are printed on linen cover stock with matching envelopes.

The prints include the Cape Elizabeth Light, Portland Head Light, Pemaquid Point Light, Rockland Breakwater Light, Dice Head Light, the Bass Harbor Head Light, Frenchman's Bay, The Sardine Cannery, The Lobster Dealer, and the Marshall Point Lighthouse.

Unmatted prints are $5.00. Matted prints are $10.00. A set of six unmatted prints is $25.00. The notecards come in packages of twelve with two cards of each scene. Each pack is $5.95.

Beacon Bills' retail outlet is at 228 Main Street in Bar Harbor. Summer hours are daily from 9:00 A.M. to 6:00 P.M. Off season hours are Monday through Saturday from 12:00 P.M. to 5:00 P.M.

Free brochure. Wholesale available. Goods stocked and shipped within one week by UPS or U.S. mail. Payment by MasterCard, Visa, check, or money order.

Brookfield Craft Center

P. O. Box 122
Route 25
Brookfield, Connecticut 06804
(203) 775-4526

Brookfield Craft Center, a non-profit center dedicated to "promoting and preserving the skills of the American craftsman," offers more than 300 workshops a year to amateur and professional artists. Workshops are taught by nationally acclaimed artists and craftsmen, making it one of the finest non-academic schools for professional study in America.

Besides such traditional crafts as ceramics, weaving, metalsmithing, woodworking, and stained glass, the Center offers many other courses, including boat building, computer use, home building and restoration, photography, design theory, and business and marketing for artists. The Center has a scholarship program for teachers and students.

For students and craftsmen who cannot visit the Connecticut campus, the Brookfield Video Library provides top-quality craft education tapes for home study and reference. Each tape has an expert craftsperson showing the step-by-step details of an artistic project. The tape library will be expanded every year.

The two tapes currently available are "Traditional New England Basketmaking with John McGuire" ($69.95), and "The Complete Metalsmith" with Tim McCreight" ($39.95).

The gallery, shops, and mail order service feature handmade works by more than 500 artists, linking the public to the heritage of fine American craftsmanship.

Galleries and shops are located on the campuses.

Free catalog. Wholesale available. Goods are stocked with some made to order. Shipped UPS within two weeks. Will ship to Canada. Payment by American Express, MasterCard, Visa, check, or money order.

Courses			
Building and Remodeling Your Home	$ 85.00	Hot Glass Workshop	140.00
Interior Design Workshop	210.00	Jewelry Making	165.00
Gilding and Gold Leaf	140.00	Champleve and Cloisonne Enameling	140.00
Introduction to Basketry	210.00	Bookbinding Workshop	140.00
Carving and Painting a Working Decoy	140.00	Basic Camera and Printing Workshop	140.00
Ceramics on the Wheel	210.00	Studio Photography Workshop	140.00
On Loom Weaving	210.00	The Business of Photography	140.00
Banners, Flags, and Sky Art	140.00	European Style Cabinets	170.00
Quilts and Illusion Workshop	85.00	Japenese Joinery	140.00
Kasuri-Shifted Weft Ikat	140.00	Eighteenth Century Carving Techniques	140.00
The Amish and Their Quilts	$140.00	Furniture Construction Workshop	140.00

The Christmas Tree Barn

48B Cold River Road
North Clarendon, Vermont 05759
(802) 775-4585

The Buck Family's Christmas Tree Barn is a 150-year-old antique barn with a slate roof and pegged beams that once sheltered great-Grandfather Buck's Belgian draft horses. A shop now stands where the horses once stamped snow off their hooves after a day spent in the woods hauling maple sap. Where the team's harnesses and sleighbells once hung, the scent of balsam and pine boughs mixes with that of hot mulled cider and spices brewing atop a wood stove. In addition to the maple trees and flowers that grow on the 140-acre farm, there are hundreds of Christmas trees that have been growing since Grandfather Ray Cary Buck discontinued dairy farming.

The decor of the Christmas Tree Barn is reminiscent of a country store. It is filled with antiques, quality hand-created gifts, dried flowers, and Christmas ornaments and decorations. They specialize in gifts that reflect the romance of their European and colonial American heritage, and they take great pride in their special custom designs. Much time is spent in the creation of decorations designed to match your lifestyle and the decor of your home or business. And they have a special selection of wedding items, from dried floral creations appropriate for wedding bouquets to hats and headpieces.

All of this is available through their catalog, from the balsam wreaths to the Christmas trees, from the Victorian-style gifts made from dried flowers and ribbons to the gift baskets filled with a selection of spices, jams, flowers, potpourri, maple syrup, and Christmas ornaments. Use their Augusta Nosegay ($8.00), a fluff of ecru lace surrounding a miniature bouquet of dried flowers, as a table favor or small corsage. Hang up a satin and lace Victorian Potpourri Kissing Ball ($18.00) made with a delightful strawberry fragrance.

Don't miss their special small gifts, country memories, Christmas collectibles, tree trims, and barn classics sections of the catalog.

Free catalog. Products guaranteed. Price quotes by letter or phone. Most goods are stocked; some made to order. Shipped UPS within two weeks. Will ship to Canada. Payment by American Express, MasterCard, Visa, check, or money order.

WHERE TRADITION BEGINS

Gingerbear	$30.00
Tussie Mussie Nosegay	15.00
Memorabilia Swag	12.00
Vermont Cow Basket	20.00
Musical Doll	26.50
Deluxe Decorated Wreath	29.95
Miniature Decorated Tree	37.00
Bay Leaf Wreath	20.00

The Crockett Collection

P. O. 1428
Manchester Center, Vermont 05255
(802) 362-2913

Since 1929, the Crockett Collection has been handcrafting beautifully silkscreened greeting cards. They offer the unusual touch of truly creative artists and the skill of accomplished craftspeople who create smart, elegant designs suitable for framing.

The silkscreen process is a stencil method of printing. A stencil is adhered to fine mesh cloth that is stretched tightly over a wooden frame. Ink is pressed through the mesh openings of the screen not blocked by the stencil.

Considerable time and skill goes into each card to create the extraordinary beauty of the silkscreened print. From their wide selection of designs you can choose one that best suits your heritage or hobbies. Personalized cards are also available.

Pick the rustic barn shrouded in a peaceful snowfall and home to a flock of doves. Or how about the tiny sailboat hanging from a tree or Santa peacefully sleeping inside a treble clef sign. And there's the partridge sitting in a pear wreath, the elaborate carousel horse, or the playful whale. Or the church at night, with the yellow glow of its window reflecting out over the

falling snow. You can almost hear the carols drifting softly through the night.

The Crockett Collection has a retail shop on Route 7 North, in Manchester Center. It is open Monday through Saturday from 10:00 A.M. to 5:00 P.M. Call for Sunday hours.

Free catalog. Wholesale available. Price quotes sometimes given, by letter or phone. Minimum order of $20.00. Products guaranteed. Goods in stock and shipped within two weeks by UPS. Will ship to Canada. Payment by check only.

DeLorme Mapping Company

P. O. Box 298
Freeport, Maine 04032
(207) 865-4171
(800) 227-1656, ext. 6850
(800) 462-0029, ext. 6850 (inside Maine)

In 1975 David DeLorme saw the need for a detailed atlas of Maine with back roads and recreational features. Today, that atlas is the best-selling book in the state of Maine and has paved the way for the Atlas and Gazetteer Series.

These quality 11" x 15" atlases of individual states give an intimate look at the geography of each state. They show back roads, trails, all lakes, ponds, streams, mountains, hills, and marshes. The gazetteers describe and/or locate hiking tours, canoe trips, campgrounds, boat ramps, and other recreational opportunities and points of interest. Available for $12.95 each, plus $3.00 for UPS shipping for the first atlas and $.25 shipping for each additional one.

Atlases	
Florida	Pennsylvania
Maine ($11.95)	Vermont ($11.95)
Michigan	Tennessee
Minnesota	Virginia
New Hampshire ($11.95)	Washington
New York	Wisconsin
Northern California	(Other states will be
Ohio	available in the near future.
Southern California	Call for availability.)

DeLorme also publishes canoeing books, nature prints, calendars, and an extensive selection of Maine and New Hampshire maps and guide books. The retail store is on Route 1 in Freeport, and is open Monday through Saturday from 9:00 A.M. to 5:00 P.M.

"When it comes to the outdoors . . . we show the way."

Write or call for a free catalog. Wholesale available for resale only. All products are guaranteed. Ships UPS within 48 hours to the United States and Canada. Accepts American Express, MasterCard, Visa, checks, or money order.

F. H. Gillingham and Sons' Vermont General Store

16 Elm Street
Woodstock, Vermont 05091
(800) 344-6668

I n 1886, F. H. Gillingham opened a small general store with one goal in mind: to offer his customers "your money's worth or your money back." His store and his family expanded, and F. H.'s sons carried on the family business.

Today, F. H.'s great-grandson Jireh still keeps his customers in his mind as he stocks the store with the finest Vermont products made. Maple syrup and traditional maple leaf candy, hand-thrown pottery and ash baskets, nostalgic items such as food tins, cast iron accessories, penny candy, and freshly ground coffee. Their catalog holds a wealth of gift suggestions for holidays or just for fun.

Free catalog. Goods stocked and shipped UPS within two weeks. Will ship to Canada. Products guaranteed. Payment by American Express, MasterCard, Visa, check, or money order.

Like any general store, F. H. Gillingham and Sons carries too many things to list. Some of their more interesting items are:

Maple Syrup	1 pint	$12.95
Salmon Falls Pottery	Cream	19.95
Wrought Iron Paper Towel Holder		27.50
Cow Cutting Board	8" x 12"	17.50
Shaker Basket	8" x 10"	27.95
Nostalgia Tins	Set of 5	22.95
Steam Pudding Mold	2-quart	135.00

Bennington Potters Stoneware has been made in Vermont since 1948.

Harpswell Press

132 Water Street
Gardiner, Maine 04345
(207) 582-1899

Harpswell Press publishes stories of Maine, of people who have worked hard and struggled to maintain a tradition, stories of a way of life Down East. Originally located in Harpswell, Maine, Harpswell Press is now in downtown Gardiner. They have eighteen books in print. The subjects range from canoe construction, photography, and Maine humor to essays on country living and country cooking. All of their authors live in Maine, but the books have an appeal that stretches far beyond the state's borders.

Free catalog. Books are distributed both retail and wholesale. Goods are stocked and shipped the day the order is received. Shipped by UPS or U. S. mail, according to customer preference. Will ship to Canada. Payment by MasterCard, Visa, check, or money order.

The Tinker of Salt Cove, by Susan Hand Shetterly. Juvenile-Young Adult. $13.95.

Different Waterfronts: Stories from the Wooden Boat Revival, by Peter H. Spectre. $22.95.

Message Through Time: The Photographs of Emma D. Sewall 1836-1919, by Abbie Sewall. $21.95/paper. $49.95/hardcover.

Have You Ever Noticed That Rabbits Don't Sing? by Nina Medina. Children's. $7.95.

What's Cooking At Moody's Diner: 60 Years of Recipes and Reminiscences, by Nancy Genthner. $8.95.

The Maritime History of Maine, by William Hutchinson Rowe. $14.95.

Pink Chimneys: A Novel of Nineteenth Century Maine, by Ardeana Hamlin Knowles. $9.95.

Postcards From Maine, by Tim Sample. $8.95.

Saturday Night at Moody's Diner and Other Stories, by Tim Sample. $8.95.

The Wood and Canvas Canoe, by Jerry Stelmok and Rollin Thurlow. $17.95.

Seacoast Maine: People and Places, by Martin Dibner. $17.95.

So You Think You Know Maine: The Board Game. $14.95.

So You Think You Know Maine, by Neil Rolde and WCBB. $13.95.

That Yankee Cat: The Maine Coon, by Marilis Hornidge. $8.95.

From the Orange Mailbox: Notes from a Few Country Acres, by A. Carman Clark. $10.95/paper. $16.95/hardcover.

Maine Bassin', by Harry Vanderweide and Dave Barnes. $13.95.

The Maine Sportsman Complete Guide to Hunting, edited by Harry Vanderweide. $14.95.

Moose Stew, by Herbert F. Goodwin. $19.95.

Whalemen and Whaleships of Maine, by Kenneth R. Martin. $7.95.

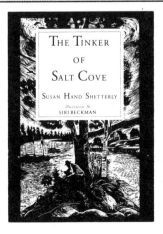

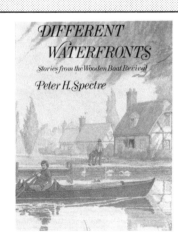

Hawk Folio

RR #1, Box 182 B
Perkinsville, Vermont 05151
(802) 263-9400

New England has long been known for the fine quality of it traditional arts and crafts. It is also home to some of the most innovative and artistic contemporary designers and craftspeople in America.

For instance, Josh Simpson's blown glass creations have been exhibited in the Smithsonian, the Carnegie Mellon Museum, and the Cooper-Hewitt Museum.

Peter Maynard, who has been making furniture since he was 17, apprenticed with several Connecticut furniture makers and now makes high-quality reproductions. He has a line of his own designs.

Tanya Laurer handpaints modern and unique designs on charmeuse and crêpe de chine silk. Her dolman tops are a striking addition to any wardrobe.

Hawk Folio offers the finest quality works from some of the country's most exciting artists and craftspeople. Clothing and jewelry, pottery, dinnerware, wooden toys, limited edition prints, quilts, and fine custom created furniture for the home are all included. They will also accept requests for custom work from the artists they list.

The current Hawk Folio lists almost 200 artisans. Each item in the catalog is made to order, so most items require two to five weeks to be hand finished to your specifications.

Free catalog. Discounts available to interior designers and architects. Price quotes on custom orders only, by letter or phone. Products guaranteed. Most items shipped UPS; larger items, such as furniture, shipped by common carrier. Will ship to Canada. Payment by American Express, MasterCard, Visa, check, or money order.

Item	Artist	Price
Cherry Storage Trunk	Geo. F. Kratz	$ 950.00
Mahogany Gaming Table	William Brooks	12,500.00
"Mega-Worlds" Paperweight	Josh Simpson	260.00
Cotton Rag Rug	Marcia Hammond	145.00
Chinese Rosewood Table	Peter Maynard	11,000.00
Handpainted Silk Dolman Top	Tanya Laurer	74.00
Art Deco Music Stand	James McDonald	1400.00
Porcelain Dinnerware Set	Joseph Triplo	88.00
Sheepskin Coat	Cindy Spolek	780.00
Porcelain Raku Tray	Dina Angel-Wing	68.00

Archblocks and Wooden Farm Tractor and Trailer

Blue New Mexico Perfume Bottle

Heartwood School

Johnson Road
Washington, Massachusetts 01235
(413) 623-6677

In 1978 a school was founded to teach the skills and knowledge it takes to build an energy-efficient house. The Heartwood courses are designed to be useful to a skilled builder as well as the novice. Their comprehensive house building courses last three weeks; specialized courses are one week.

Heartwood believes students learn by doing, and the housebuilding courses are based on a program of participation interspersed with classroom instruction. Students use models and full-scale mock-ups of house frames to see the steps involved in framing a house. They then work on actually framing a section of a house with an experienced builder.

The housebuilding course includes an introduction to tools, vocabulary, materials, power tool use and safety practices, site preparation, solar orientation, foundation types and how to build them, structural principles, calculating timber sizes, building code requirements, framing systems, roof framing and finishing, insulation and vapor barriers, options for interior and exterior finishes, installing doors and windows, building stairs, and plumbing and electrical systems.

The three-week housebuilding courses are $800.00 per person or $1400.00 per couple. The one-week courses are $375.00 per person or $650 per couple, and include Contracting, Renovation, Cabinetmaking, Timberframing, Finish Carpentry, Carpentry for Women, and Masonry.

The people who come to Heartwood include teachers, truck drivers, architects, social workers, retirees, real estate agents, and high school students. Most have little or no previous construction experience, but they all share a clear determination to empower their hands, to train their eyes for quality and beauty in design, and to question and explore the ways they might live in a more honest relationship with the planet.

Courses start in mid-April and run through the first week in October.

Call or write for a free catalog. Payment for courses can be made by check or money order.

HEARTWOOD

L. L. Bean

Freeport, Maine 04033-0001
(800) 221-4221

It all started because L. L. Bean hated having wet feet. An avid hunter, he would not stay out of the woods, but he was continually frustrated by shoes that wouldn't keep his feet dry. Finally, he got the idea of making a soft leather upper shoe and sewing it to a regular pair of galoshes. They worked great. L.L., who was a partner in his brother's dry-goods store, decided to go into the mail order business.

He sold one hundred pairs of his new boots, promising a 100 percent guarantee. When ninety pairs came back because the stitching pulled out of the soft rubber of the galoshes, L.L. stuck by his guarantee and scraped together the money for the refunds. Then he persuaded the U.S. Rubber Company in Boston to manufacture a better sole and sent out new flyers. The boots were a hit.

L.L. was selling more than just a boot. He was selling his name, his reliability. Customers could trust him. His guarantee was upheld no matter what. If those soles pulled out after twenty-five years, you could still get them replaced. That guarantee is still the L.L. Bean way of doing business, and it has brought them from a one item mail order company founded in 1912, to a major retail and mail order operation that sends out more than 116 million catalogs every year, and in 1989 did $600 million in sales.

Yet dealing with L.L. Bean is not like dealing with a major corporation. In most ways, it's still like dealing with L.L.'s dry goods store. The customer service employees go through eight days of training before they ever talk to a customer, and they often have experience with most of the products. They do everything possible to create customer loyalty. Customers call just to chat or ask advice on what to take camping or if sending their children to Outward Bound is a good idea. Catalog models are all company employees and their children and pets.

L.L. Bean is like a major corporation in some ways, though. Manufacturing a lot of the items ensures the finest quality products. The catalogs feature a huge selection of products, from L.L.'s original Maine Hunting Shoe, to clothes for casual, dress, or rugged outdoor wear. The most popular items in the L.L. Bean catalog include boat and tote bags, chamois cloth shirts, sleeping bags, tents, knapsacks, Baxter State parkas, dog beds, scotch plaid shirts, and Blucher moccasins and other handsewn footwear. And because so many items are available, the prices are competitive and affordable.

You can rely on L.L. Bean. That's not just a guarantee; it's their way of doing business.

Free catalog. Products guaranteed. Goods stocked and shipped UPS or U.S. mail. Priority Mail and Federal Express service available. Order usually filled within 24 hours. Will ship to Canada. Payment by American Express, MasterCard, Visa, check, or money order.

L.L.Bean®

Made the Maine Way

P. O. Box 639/21 Elm Street
Camden, Maine 04843
(800) 242-2884 (outside Maine)
(800) 244-2884 (inside Maine)

The philosophy of Made the Maine Way is that each craft carries a little something of the craftsperson with it, making each item unique. They have put together a selection of the best Maine crafts available.

By taking care of the communication with the customer, Made the Maine Way allows Maine craftspeople to concentrate on their art. Whenever possible, the customers receive their purchase with full understanding of the person who created it. From sweaters, baskets, and pottery, to lobsters, cheese and candies, they offer the best of Maine.

Made the Maine Way operates a retail shop on the corner of Elm and Washington streets in downtown Camden, open during the summer from 9:00 A.M. to 9:00 P.M. Another shop is located in Boothbay at the Spruce Point Inn. Call for hours.

Item	Creator	Price
Loon Doorstops	Heritage Metal Crafts	$42.00
Maine Rockers	Don Moore	57.00
Danica Design Candles	Eric and Cindy Lausten	9.00/pr.
Kat's Baskets	Kathy Tarbet	40.00
Skowhegan Handwoven Rag Rugs	Susan Blaisdell	48.50
Sunbower Earthy Organics Pottery	Denise Yeamons	18.00/mug

Free catalog and shipping. Goods stocked, some custom pieces. Product guaranteed. Shipped within three weeks by UPS or U.S. mail on request. Will ship to Canada. Payment by MasterCard, Visa, check, or money order.

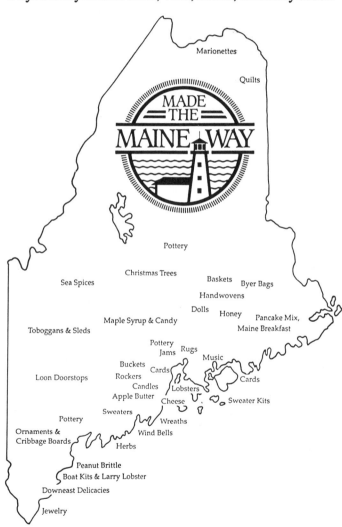

Maine Line Products

11 Main Street, Box 356
Bethel, Maine 04217
(207) 824-2522

Richard and Ellen Whitney, owners of Maine Line Products, spend a lot of time searching for unique and interesting products that reflect both pride in craftsmanship and pride in a New England heritage.

The Maine Woodman's Weatherstick, a rustic weather predictor, was one of their finds and Richard and Ellen have been selling it for more than ten years. They swear it really works. Hang the weatherstick on an outside wall or door casing exposed to the weather. The stick bends down to foretell foul weather and up for fair. It's only $4.95, or you can get 3 for $12.00 (plus shipping).

Maine Line Products also sells wooden toys, including a train made of rugged birch and pine, and tops

that spin forever. They have a hardwood Shaker peg rack and wooden baskets. Among their best selling products are their rustic birch bird houses. Most products are under $25.00, and they contain a wealth of craftsmanship and regional pride.

The Maine Line Products retail shop is on Main Street in Bethel. Hours are Monday through Saturday from 9:00 A.M. to 5:00 P.M.

Free catalog. Wholesale available. Price quotes by letter only. Products guaranteed. Goods are stocked and shipped UPS or U. S. Mail. Shipping time varies. Will ship to Canada. Payment by American Express, MasterCard, Visa, check, or money order. Credit cards accepted on retail order only.

24-inch Hardwood Shaker Peg Rack	$ 7.00
16" x 14" x 12 " Wooden Basket	9.95
Mr. Moose Wall Hanging	24.95
Pin-up Lamp With Shade	9.95
Large Wooden Train	8.95
Small Wooden Train	5.00
Doll's Rocking Chair	15.00
36-inch Hobby Horse (with wheel)	9.95
Wooden Toy Top	.50
Birch Bird House	19.95
Candle Lamp with Candle	9.95

"Maine Made Gifts"

Maine Line Products

Marie Boucher Designs

326 Elm Street
Biddeford, Maine 04005
(207) 284-6701

Hand-lettered calligraphy prints from Marie Boucher Designs make you pause during a busy day and think about the true joys of life—love, the laughter of children, the fresh smell of a breeze from the shore. These usually brief words capture the essence of our desires, our caring.

Now you can take these words and hang them in your home or set them on your desk at work.

All Marie Boucher Designs prints contain individually hand-illuminated touches, making every piece an original. Different techniques, such as stenciling, watercolor, and handpressed dried flowers, are used to add personal touches. They present each piece either matted and framed or matted and shrink-wrapped.

Marie Boucher Designs also offers two handmade accordian books filled with silk-screened calligraphy and covered with original hand-marbled paper. These books are hand illuminated with watercolors, and tied with pure silk ribbons. A solid brass display easel is available.

They use only soft country colors such as blue, dusty rose, colonial orange, pewter, green, and off-white, which complement all their styles.

The designs come in a variety of sizes. The dried flower pieces measure 4" x 5", the stenciled pieces measure 5" x 7", 8" x 10", and 11" x 14". The books are 4" x 4¼" and the brass easel is 7" high.

Prices range from $15.50 for a matted and shrink-wrapped 5" x 7" print to $62.00 for a 12" x 16" framed print.

Catalog available for $4.00, refundable with purchase. Wholesale available. Price quotes available for custom work only, by letter. Products guaranteed. Most goods stocked, some made to order. Shipped within two weeks by UPS. Will ship to Canada. Retail orders prepaid only, by check or money order.

MARIE BOUCHER
GRAPHIC DESIGN STUDIO
& GALLERY

Betty Ann Maynard Handpainted Originals

Box 225R
East Boothbay, Maine 04544
(207) 633-2399

The Maynards were a typical American family with children, school, work, a busy life with summers in Ocean Point, Maine. Although Betty Ann had studied art in school, she painted only on a limited basis until the kids were grown. It was then she discovered that the love of the coast that she had developed during those Ocean Point summers was going to reap more than just memories—Betty Ann started painting more extensively.

Her delicate drawings are loving vignettes of life on the Maine coast. Elegant ships, rustic landscapes, detailed wildlife, and plants are her subjects, and she carefully handpaints each note card and print. Prints are signed, matted and ready to frame; note-cards are carefully packaged with high-quality envelopes.

Betty Ann designs cards for everyday, for Christmas, or for an individualized gift. A pack of six note cards with envelopes is $7.00. A matted 5" x 7" print is also $7.00. Matted 8" x 10" prints available for $12.50. Bulk quantities of note-cards are also available for $95.00 per 100. All postpaid.

Free brochure with sample. Wholesale available. Price quotes on special orders only by letter. Goods stocked and shipped by UPS or U.S. mail within three weeks. Payment by check or money order. Mail orders must be prepaid.

The Orvis Company

Rt. 7A
Manchester Vermont 05254
(800) 548-9548

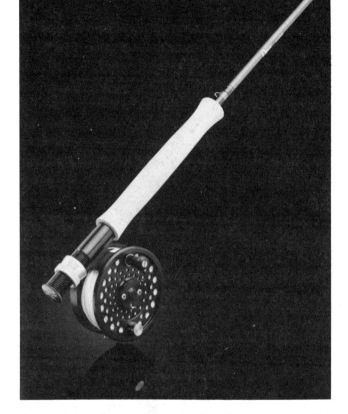

America's oldest mail order company also has the largest selection of fly-fishing products in the world.

Established in 1856 by Charles F. Orvis, the company handcrafts graphite, boron-graphite and bamboo fly rods in Manchester. Although the company has expanded and now offers hunting gear, country gifts, classic men's and women's clothing, the fly rods are still their featured item and each rod carries a 25-year guarantee.

Silk Blend Handknit Cardigan	$ 49.00
Women's Tweed Jacket	158.00
Madras Buttondown Shirts	30.00
8 Foot 9 Inch Bonefisher Boron/Graphite Rod	525.00
Battenkill® Bamboo Rod	1,215.00
Adjustable Fly Box Case	35.00
Orvis Skirted Spool Spin Reel	60.00

ORVIS®

Free catalog. Products stocked and guaranteed. Shipped by UPS or Federal Express. Will ship to Canada. Payment by American Express, MasterCard, Visa, money order.

Retail Outlets

142 East Ontario
Chicago, IL 60611
(312) 440-0662

45th St. Between
Madison and Vanderbilt
New York, NY 10017
(212) 697-3133

8605 Germantown Ave.
Chestnut Hill, PA 19118
(215) 242-9332

5848 Westheimer Rd.
Houston, TX 77057
(713) 783-2111

Conservatory #070
800 Nicollet Mall
Minneapolis, MN 55402
(612) 339-5409

1423 Walnut St.
Philadelphia, PA 19102
(215) 567-6207

Historic Route 7A
Manchester, VT 05254
(802) 362-3750

27 Sackville St.
in the West End
London, England
W1X 1DA
01-494-2660

300 Grant Avenue
San Francisco, CA 94108
(415) 392-1600

The Orvis Shop at Bridge
House, High Street
Stockbridge, Hant, England
Andover (0264) 810-017

19 Campbell Avenue
Roanoke, VA 24010
(703) 345-3635

Saltbox Studio of Maine

RR1, Box 2570
North Edgecomb, Maine 04556
(207) 633-6657

Saltbox Studio makes and sells "Yestertoys," which are produced for decorative purposes, not as playthings for children. Their toy list includes a Noah's Ark set, a pulltoy pony, a miniature train, and an 1850 cradle. The Maine Wooly-Lamb is a pulltoy reproduction wrapped in bulky wool from Harmony, Maine. The Hired Girl's Rope Bed has a hand-stenciled heart design and is just the right size for a special doll or teddy bear.

Saltbox Studio has recently added a "Belted Barnyard," three black and white pulltoys—a Galloway cow, Hampshire pig, and Dutch rabbit.

On the more "adult" list are decorative maple sugar molds, Maine Woods backgammon board, and binocular box, which is a featured product at the Maine Audubon Society Headquarters Gift Shop in Falmouth. The binocular box was Saltbox Studio's first creation. Decorated with stenciled ducks, and lined with soft felt, it holds standard-size binoculars with room for a bird book. Two other items are an herb drying rack and a wildflower press. Most items are under $25.00.

Free catalog with SASE. Wholesale available. Price quotes by letter only. Products shipped by UPS or U.S. mail within two weeks. Will ship to Canada. Payment by MasterCard, Visa, check, or money order. Products also available at seven selected craft fairs.

Thornton W. Burgess Museum

4 Water Street
Sandwich, Massachusetts 02563
(508) 888-6870

Peter Rabbit, the story animal beloved by generations of children, was created in Sandwich by a naturalist concerned that children be taught about nature.

In memory of Mr. Burgess' concerns, the museum offers a wide selection of items to promote interest in wildlife and the natural environment. Along with the fine crystal, ceramic, and marble collectibles, are special editions of Mr. Burgess' books, T-shirts, and toys.

The museum operates a retail shop, open Monday through Saturday from 10:00 A.M. to 4:00 P.M., and Sunday from 1:00 P.M. to 4:00 P.M.

Free catalog. Wholesale available. No price quotes. Goods stocked and shipped within four weeks by UPS. Will ship to Canada. Payment by MasterCard, Visa, or check.

Burgess Animal Character Sweatshirts	Adults	$13.95
	Children	12.95
Plush Animals— Large Owl		19.95
Bunny Hand Puppets		11.95
Fox		11.50
Baby Sack		10.95
Wooden Cup Plate Frames	3-Plate	12.00
	4-Plate	15.00
Herbal Cup Plates		7.95
Whale Cup Plates		7.95
Ceramic Birds		8.00
Artefice Ottanta (Crushed marble birds)		16.95

The Vermont Country Store

P. O. Box 3000
Manchester Center, Vermont 05255
(802) 362-2400

Have you ever wondered where you could buy an original McGuffey's Reader? How about an 8' by 13½' world map, or Sal Hepatica Original Powder? Remember those 1950s pastel lawn chairs with the shell backs, and the hand-push reel lawn mower? Did you ever think you would see another floursack towel?

When Gardner Lyman opened his store in North Calais, Vermont, in 1897, his business philosophy was simple: "Don't ever let the notion that our country store should peddle souvenirs to city folks creep into your head. Go find the products that solve your customers' problems."

Gardner's grandson, Lyman Orton, still follows that advice. The Vermont Country Store has been operating a mail order service since 1946, dedicated to providing useful and often hard-to-find items for its

customers. They sell maple syrup or penny candy, natural fabric clothing, personal care items, or a typewriter. If you need it, all you have to do is ask.

The Vermont Country Store operates two retail shops: one on Route 100 in Weston (802) 824-3184, and one on Route 103 in Rockingham (802) 463-2224. Their mail order office is (802) 362-2400.

Free catalog. Goods stocked and shipped UPS or U.S. mail within 48 hours. Will ship to Canada. No price quotes. Payment by MasterCard, Visa, check, or money order.

Lyman Orton and the Vermont Country Store's
8' x 13 ½' World Map

Shell Back Gliders	$115.00
1938 Loop & Tuft Cotton Reversible Rug	22.95
Goose Feather Pillow	16.50
Log Cabin Tier Country Lace Curtain	19.95
Irish Linen Handkerchiefs	15.00/2
Reversible Cotton Jersey Dress	62.50
Old Maine Trotters Pumps	55.00
McGuffey's Readers Set	44.95
Natural Herb Moth Repellent	9.95/8
Refrigerator Drawer Liners	8.00/4
Lotil Cream For Cracked and Sore Fingers	7.50
Dominica Bay Rum After-Bath Lotion	9.95
Faux-Tortoise Hairpins	10.80/12
Hand-Push Reel Mower	89.95
Tibet Almond Furniture Scratch Stick	5.90/2
English Rockingham Teapot	16.95
100% Cotton Floursack Towels	9.60/6
Lemon Drop	6.50/2 lbs.
Vermont Common Crackers	5.25

APPENDIX ONE

ALPHABETICAL LISTING
OF COMPANIES BY STATE

Massachusetts

New Hampshire

Rhode Island

Vermont

APPENDIX TWO

ALPHABETICAL LISTING OF COMPANIES

INDEX

We are now planning a second edition of *New England By Mail*. If you would like your company considered for inclusion, please write to the editor:

Ms. Ramona Richards
Rutledge Hill Press
513 Third Avenue South
Nashville, TN 37210

There is no charge to be included in *New England By Mail*. Selection of companies is at the editor's and compilers' discretion and based on the uniqueness of products, their quality, the company's reputation, and its service.